Katherine Muncaster
Steve Oakes

Mental Toughness

Practical classroom activities to help young people cope with stress, challenge and change

RISING STARS

The Publishers would like to thank the following for permission to reproduce copyright material.

Photocredits

Classroom photos © Katherine Muncaster

p23 © Pikovit/Adobe Stock; p40 © Laura Pashkevich/Adobe Stock; p52 © Nutkins, J./Adobe Stock; p57 © Rawpixel/Adobe Stock; p61 left © Mark Stay/Adobe Stock, right © strekalova/Adobe Stock; p102 © EVERST/Adobe Stock; p105 © kolonko/Adobe Stock; p139 © v_ctoria/Adobe Stock; p151 top © Lightfield Studios/Adobe Stock, bottom © zimmytws/Adobe Stock; p152 © New Africa/Adobe Stock; p162 © tomertu/Adobe Stock; p170 © Moving Moment/Adobe Stock; p182 © jamesteohart/Adobe Stock

Acknowledgements

Every effort has been made to trace all copyright holders, but if any have been inadvertently overlooked, the Publishers will be pleased to make the necessary arrangements at the first opportunity.

Although every effort has been made to ensure that website addresses are correct at time of going to press, Rising Stars cannot be held responsible for the content of any website mentioned in this book. It is sometimes possible to find a relocated web page by typing in the address of the home page for a website in the URL window of your browser.

Hachette UK's policy is to use papers that are natural, renewable and recyclable products and made from wood grown in well-managed forests and other controlled sources. The logging and manufacturing processes are expected to conform to the environmental regulations of the country of origin.

Orders: Please contact Hachette UK Distribution, Hely Hutchinson Centre, Milton Road, Didcot, Oxfordshire, OX11 7HH. Telephone: +44 (0)1235 400555. Lines are open from 9 a.m. to 5 p.m., Monday to Friday. Email primary@hachette.co.uk

Visit our website at www.risingstars-uk.com for details of the full range of Rising Stars publications.

Online support and queries email: onlinesupport@risingstars-uk.com

ISBN: 978 1 3983 5447 0

© Hodder & Stoughton Limited 2023

First published in 2023 by
Hodder & Stoughton Limited (for its Rising Stars imprint, part of the Hodder Education Group)
An Hachette UK Company
Carmelite House
50 Victoria Embankment
London EC4Y 0DZ

www.risingstars-uk.com

Impression number   10 9 8 7 6 5 4 3 2 1

Year   2027 2026 2025 2024 2023

All rights reserved. Apart from any use permitted under UK copyright law, no part of this publication may be reproduced or transmitted in any form or by any means, electronic or mechanical, including photocopying and recording, or held within any information storage and retrieval system, without permission in writing from the publisher or under licence from the Copyright Licensing Agency Limited. Further details of such licences (for reprographic reproduction) may be obtained from the Copyright Licensing Agency Limited, www.cla.co.uk

Typeset in India by Aptara Inc.

Printed in Italy

A catalogue record for this title is available from the British Library.

MIX
Paper | Supporting responsible forestry
FSC
www.fsc.org
FSC™ C104740

Contents

How to use this book	1
The Mental Toughness Framework	8

Sessions for 4–5-year-olds (Reception) — 15

1	I am good at …	18
2	Inside me	22
3	Trying again	26
4	Too small	29
5	Bounce	33
6	New challenges	36
7	Stickability	40
8	Choices	45

Sessions for 5–6-year-olds (Year 1) — 49

1	Wall of strength	51
2	I can't do it!	54
3	Giant steps	57
4	Stickability	60
5	Being great	63
6	Words, words, words	65
7	Power of mistakes	68
8	My 4Cs	71

Sessions for 6–7-year-olds (Year 2) — 74

1	Burst the bubble!	76
2	Step by step	79
3	My bank of strength	83
4	Stuck	86
5	We are all different	89
6	I believe I can	92
7	Pop, fizz, pop, fizz	95
8	I excel at …	98

Sessions for 7–8-year-olds (Year 3) — 100

1. I have learnt to … — 102
2. Worry spectrum — 105
3. Looking at things differently — 108
4. Yet — 111
5. A really hard thing — 115
6. You choose — 120
7. Erupting — 126
8. Perfect recipe — 130

Sessions for 8–9-year-olds (Year 4) — 133

1. My remote control – managing worries — 136
2. Dominoes of learning — 139
3. I am awesome — 142
4. Tough guys — 146
5. Building our inner strength — 150
6. Committed to … — 154
7. Comfort zone — 158
8. My wish — 162

Sessions for 9–10-year-olds (Year 5) — 165

1. What I am thankful for … — 167
2. Marshmallow test — 170
3. Help me — 174
4. Stickability — 178
5. On track — 182
6. Network audit — 185
7. Just a minute — 188
8. Agony Aunt — 191

Sessions for 10–11-year-olds (Year 6) — 195

1. I am unique — 197
2. Myth of intelligence — 200
3. Circles of control — 204
4. Going with the flow — 208
5. Passion project — 213
6. Change — 217
7. SMART goals — 221
8. Inner critic — 225

References — 228

How to use this book

Mental toughness and the 4Cs

The activities in this book are designed to provide pupils with plenty of opportunities to learn about, reflect on and discuss the 4Cs:
- control
- challenge
- commitment
- confidence.

The 4C model of mental toughness, the Mental Toughness Framework, was developed by Clough et al. (2002) and is described in more detail in the next section.

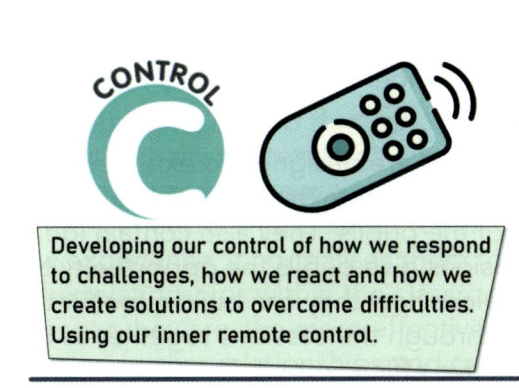

CONTROL
Developing our control of how we respond to challenges, how we react and how we create solutions to overcome difficulties. Using our inner remote control.

CHALLENGE
Wanting to challenge ourselves and trying new challenges to help ourselves grow.

COMMITMENT
Sticking at something even when it is tricky and being resilient helps us to grow.

CONFIDENCE
Identifying what we are good at and recognising this is important.

Whole-school approach

Developing a whole-school approach to mental toughness is the key for successful implementation. A key starting point is asking staff to reflect on their own mental toughness, to identify their strengths and challenges. Reflecting on your own mental toughness and life experiences enables you to approach the sessions proactively and helps to develop an effective culture.

For a whole-school approach to be truly successful, it needs to be led by all key members of staff, including the teachers and senior leadership team. This can be facilitated by whole-school assemblies that explore the 4Cs in a variety of contexts and a shared whole-school approach, for example embedding mental

Teachers as facilitators of learning

The teacher's role within the sessions is often that of a learning facilitator, but adopting this role can initially be challenging. It requires you to take a step back from being directly involved in the learning for part of the session and to listen carefully to the pupils' discussions without intervening. This will reveal a lot about the pupils' preconceptions and attitudes towards themselves and their learning. It can also provide pupils with the opportunity to discuss and reflect independently, to listen to different opinions and to resolve issues with their peers. This is an important skill for children to acquire and also encourages them to develop as independent learners.

During the pupils' discussions, it can be useful to make a note of their responses. This will allow you to share and discuss any misconceptions during feedback or to revisit at a later date.

Allow the pupils enough time to discuss each question, but not too much time that they become less focused. Monitor the pupils closely, as you want them to remain on task, with their learning developing. If they have too much time they will be distracted. To ensure they remain focused, you could use the strategy of 'eavesdropping', where you listen to the discussions from a distance, rather than intervening, and make a note of their ideas. If you have another adult in the classroom, they may act as a scribe. Then, rather than taking individual feedback, share with the class the ideas you gleaned from listening to their conversations. Ideas can also be shared through a display.

Scaffolding

Initially the sessions have been designed with clear scaffolding to support the pupils' learning, for example sorting answers into groups. However, later sessions progress to encouraging pupils to think and reflect independently, for example providing solutions to real-life scenarios and placing worries on a spectrum, which requires a unique individual response. Sessions for older pupils often contain activities where they are asked to sort ideas/concepts into two categories; however, the activity contains answers for one category only as this encourages the pupils really to think and to question the criteria rather than just quickly sort things.

The sessions also contain open-ended tasks that provide pupils with the opportunity to think and respond in their own unique way, thus encouraging and nurturing different approaches.

Preparing pupils to give feedback

Once the discussions are over, your role as teacher is to ensure that pupils have the opportunity to feed back their ideas and allow others to respond to them.

You may pre-empt any pupil who could be passive or reluctant to join in by letting them know in advance that you want to hear their ideas. Remind the pupils that there are no right or wrong ideas within these sessions and that you simply want to hear their opinions.

You could also remind the pupils that you will be randomly selecting them to share their ideas, as this will help them to focus and be active learners. Various methods can be used to select pupils randomly to give you feedback, for example you could use lollipop sticks, where each pupil's name is written on a stick and one is selected at random. Another useful alternative is to use raffle tickets where each pupil has a ticket and you select the number of a pupil to feed back, or use a bingo machine to do so. Various online resources are available where you input the pupils' names and then one is randomly selected.

Arranging the classroom

Talk partners

When pupils are working with their talk partners, it is essential that they are sitting next to each other. Pupils need to be familiar with working with a talk partner and with following simple rules (for example taking turns to speak, looking at their partner, talking about the question). These rules will vary depending on the age of the pupils and their starting points. Prior to beginning the sessions, you should remind the pupils briefly of the class success criteria for being an effective talk partner. It is useful to have a display including photographs or visual prompts that reinforce the effective characteristics.

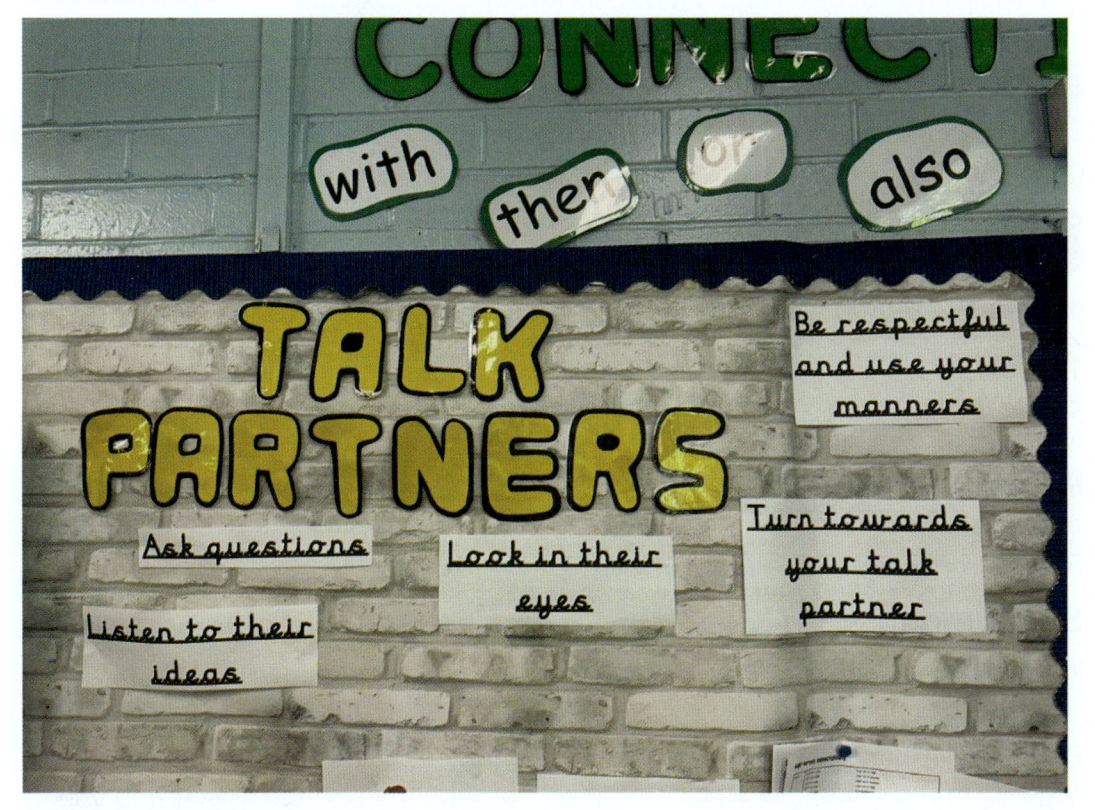

Being an effective talk partner in Year 2

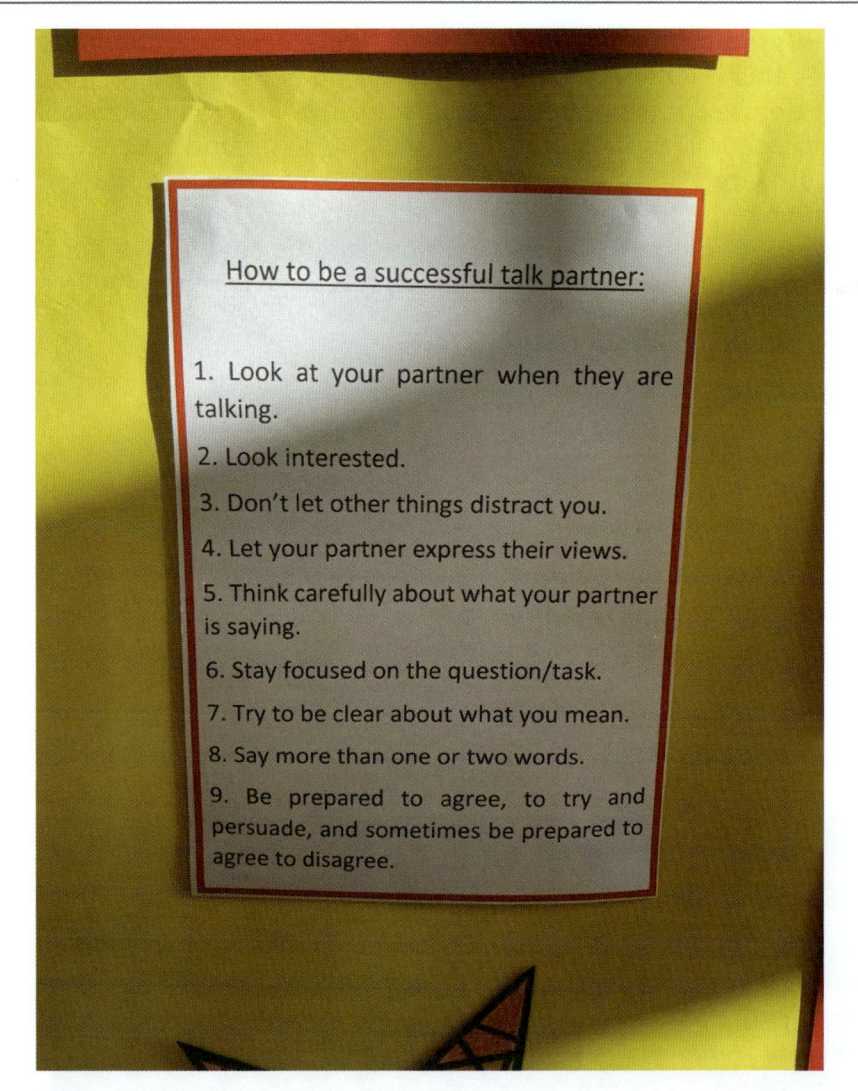

> **How to be a successful talk partner:**
>
> 1. Look at your partner when they are talking.
> 2. Look interested.
> 3. Don't let other things distract you.
> 4. Let your partner express their views.
> 5. Think carefully about what your partner is saying.
> 6. Stay focused on the question/task.
> 7. Try to be clear about what you mean.
> 8. Say more than one or two words.
> 9. Be prepared to agree, to try and persuade, and sometimes be prepared to agree to disagree.

Being an effective talk partner in Year 5

The talk partners should be changed regularly (a minimum of every two weeks but it can be weekly) as this provides the pupils with the opportunity to learn with different children.

If you have pupils who find it difficult to work co-operatively, you could ask them to talk in a group of three (with at least one member of the group acting as a good role model).

Small groups

The pupils may need to work in small groups. If it is the first time they have worked in a small group, you will need to consider the groupings carefully.

Ensure the room is set up to encourage effective discussions between the pupils. A good arrangement is a square table with pupils sitting either side facing each other. The tables could also be arranged at a slight angle so the pupils can see the board.

To encourage all the pupils to join in the discussions, an object could be passed around the group to indicate turn taking.

Use of equipment

When using any equipment, ensure that it is set up and ready to use!

It can be very helpful to use a visualiser or document camera to share a book with the pupils. This has the benefit of enabling you to zoom in on a specific image to stimulate discussion.

A camera or tablet can be used to take photographs to make cards to show key skills or to add pictures to displays.

A range of stimulus to stimulate the discussions is given throughout the book. These are available to download as PowerPoints and can be adapted and personalised to suit your context and your pupils' own experiences.

Downloadable resources

Free downloadable resources, including the 4Cs poster, teaching slides and handouts, can be found here: **bit.ly/3fOFSC1**

The myth of mental toughness

As you begin your mental-toughness journey, it is important to remember that the concept of mental toughness does not mean that the pupils should find everything easy or that they won't worry or feel emotions. Instead, it provides them with the opportunity to explore the four key concepts of control, challenge, commitment and confidence, along with a toolkit of strategies that will support them.

We hope that this book inspires you and that it supports your pupils and your school to develop both self and collective efficacy through mental toughness. We would be delighted to hear about your experiences and receive feedback on the sessions. Our contact details can be found here: **bit.ly/3fOFSC1**

The Mental Toughness Framework

The aim of this introduction is to provide an overview of the Mental Toughness Framework proposed by Professor Peter Clough and Doug Strycharczyk (2014). We think that it is important to give a fairly in-depth introduction for those of you who want to go a bit deeper into the theory and the research behind the construct of mental toughness before considering the implementation of the sessions into your school.

- We begin by exploring the concept of non-cognitive skills and some of the challenges of deciding which non-cognitive skills you might want to focus on.
- We then outline the 4C model of mental toughness as developed by Clough et al. (2002).
- Finally, we put forward some implications when considering the mental toughness approach in schools.

Non-cognitive skills

How and why does mental toughness matter? It is now widely accepted that success in education is a combination of developing knowledge, academic skills and non-cognitive factors (Farrington et al., 2012). Non-cognitive is an umbrella term for a wide-ranging set of attitudes, behaviours and strategies such as motivation and perseverance. Alternative descriptors include metacognition, soft skills, mindsets or character. The term was coined by the sociologists Bowles and Gintis (1976) in an attempt to distinguish factors other than those measured by cognitive tests, such as IQ, but was popularised by the work of Nobel Prize winner, Professor of Economics, James Heckman. Heckman has shown that early childhood development in non-cognitive skills heavily influences health, economic and social outcomes for individuals and that these are considered more important for attainment and life success than IQ (Heckman & Kautz, 2012). Yet the development of these skills in education is often left to chance or is only implicit within an individual's teaching practice.

The term 'non-cognitive' is frequently viewed as contentious as it falsely implies that these soft skills are devoid of cognition (Duckworth & Yeager, 2015). The conceptual understanding of the term 'non-cognitive' has itself made it difficult for teachers to teach non-cognitive skills in the classroom. Duckworth and Yeager (2015) prefer the term 'positive personal qualities', but this does not make implementation any more straightforward for classroom practitioners. The relationship between these skills and academic success in school-aged children is a persistent hot topic in education (Gutman & Schoon, 2013). Despite this, non-cognitive skills are largely absent from the current UK curriculum. With the lack of explicit direction from the Department for Education, educators have relied on the research and guidance provided by the Jubilee Centre for Character and Virtues at the University of Birmingham and the Education Endowment Foundation. This leaves education practitioners to identify salient non-cognitive skills from the literature, and then develop and implement interventions for use in their own context.

Two closely intertwined approaches currently favoured by teachers for developing non-cognitive skills are grit (Duckworth et al., 2007) and growth mindset (Dweck, 2006). Duckworth et al. (2007) define grit as perseverance and passion for long-term goals. One study found that grit could be improved in children as young as 4–6 years old (White et al., 2016). However, there are limitations to grit in an educational context. First, grit has only one single higher-order construct with two lower-order dimensions: 'perseverance of effort' and 'consistency of interest'. As a result, grit is often referred to as an unidimensional construct. Unidimensional constructs have limited potential in education as they omit important constructs, such as confidence, that have been shown to be related to performance and wellbeing (Stankov & Lee, 2014). Second, in their meta-analytical study, Credé et al. (2017) found that correlations with academic performance are moderate and that the construct does not appear to be all that different from conscientiousness.

An alternative approach is growth mindset: the belief that human capacities are not fixed but can be developed over time (Dweck, 2006). Pupils with growth mindsets have been found to have better academic outcomes (Blackwell et al., 2007), and a recent large-scale study (using 12,490 subjects) found a significant improvement in the grades of 14–15-year-old pupils following a growth mindset intervention (Yeager et al., 2019). However, successful implementation of school-based growth mindset interventions has been varied. A Randomised Control Trial (RCT) exploring a growth mindset intervention with 5018 10–11-year-old pupils in the UK did not find significant improvements in literacy and numeracy tests or in four measures of non-cognitive skills: intrinsic value, test anxiety, self-efficacy and self-regulation (Foliano et al., 2019). Growth mindset founder, Carol Dweck, believes that teachers commonly misinterpret the approach, with a misplaced emphasis solely on encouraging the 'effort' a pupil exhibits and using a pupil's fixed mindset as a reason for lower attainment (Dweck, 2015). Growth mindset interventions should focus on pupils adopting effective strategies, crucially to ensure that learning occurs. For more on growth mindset, see Katherine Muncaster's book: *Growth Mindset Lessons: Every Child a Learner* (Muncaster & Clarke, 2016).

The 4C model of mental toughness

Given the limitations of these approaches, a concept that combines a number of different non-cognitive skills, such as self-efficacy, conscientiousness, resilience, perseverance and buoyancy, is critical for a successful intervention in the classroom. Mental toughness is one such concept, integrating several important constructs within education including resilience, self-efficacy, confidence and motivation (McGeown et al., 2015). Several mental toughness models have been developed (e.g. Clough et al., 2002; Golby et al., 2007; Gucciardi et al., 2008). The most widely used model within education is the 4C model developed by Clough et al. (2002). The four central pillars of the 4C mental toughness model are control, challenge, commitment and confidence.

CONTROL
Developing our control of how we respond to challenges, how we react and how we create solutions to overcome difficulties. Using our inner remote control.

CHALLENGE
Wanting to challenge ourselves and trying new challenges to help ourselves grow.

COMMITMENT
Sticking at something even when it is tricky and being resilient helps us to grow.

CONFIDENCE
Identifying what we are good at and recognising this is important.

The 4C mental toughness model

The potential value of this model in an educational context has been investigated in several studies, with higher mental toughness scores correlating with academic performance (Lin et al., 2017), higher attendance / better classroom behaviour (St Clair-Thompson et al., 2015), successful high school transitions (St Clair-Thompson et al., 2017) and wellbeing (Gerber et al., 2013).

Mentally tough individuals are described as having a 'high sense of self-belief and an unshakeable faith that they can control their own destiny, these individuals can remain relatively unaffected by competition or adversity' (Clough et al., 2002, p. 38). It is worth noting that the model conceptualises the opposite end of the toughness continuum as sensitivity not weakness. This is one of the most overlooked factors for schools using the construct. It is important to stress the use of the term 'mental sensitivity' rather than 'mental weakness', and that there are advantages/challenges to being at either end of the continuum.

Mentally sensitive ⟷ Mentally tough

The continuum from mental sensitivity to mental toughness

The original mental toughness 4C model has been applied to an educational context, where the original characteristics are adapted for pupil expectations (McGeown et al., 2015).

- Control is divided into two subcomponents: life control and emotional control. Pupils with high life control feel in control of their future and those with high emotional control will be able to manage their emotions.
- Those scoring high on challenge seek out new opportunities and are open to change.
- Commitment refers to goal orientation; pupils high in commitment will enjoy setting targets or goals and are more likely to stick to them.
- Confidence is also divided into confidence in abilities and interpersonal confidence. Pupils high in confidence in ability will feel confident about attempting new things. Those with high interpersonal confidence will feel confident in social groups and are more likely to be comfortable in unfamiliar environments.

Below are some of the behaviours that could be associated with mentally tough and mentally sensitive pupils.

Mentally sensitive	Mentally tough
Don't like changes	Like challenge
Avoid effort	Enjoy hard work
Avoid answering questions	Are first to put their hand up
Like routine	Like change
Don't like to be measured	Enjoy tests
Are easily distracted	Have high levels of focus
Have an 'I can't do' attitude	Have an 'I can do' attitude
Have low self-belief	Are confident in their abilities
Don't ask questions	Are curious to find out more
Can be shy	Enjoy working in groups
Respond poorly to feedback	Seek out feedback
Feel things happen to them	Feel in control
Have trouble controlling their emotions	Stay calm
Like to be told what to do	Like to take the initiative

Behaviours associated with mentally tough and mentally sensitive pupils

The good news is that Clough and Strycharczyk (2014) argue that mental toughness is a 'plastic' personality trait and interventions delivered at key milestones in education are crucial to the development of young people. However, the genetic influence of an individual's mental toughness has raised some issues concerning malleability (Golby et al., 2007; Crust, 2008). Despite the suggestion that our genetics, to some extent, influence our mental toughness, Clough and Strycharczyk argue that there is still considerable malleability, but that the path to developing mental toughness might be easier for those who have a genetic advantage.

Interventions developed to improve the mental toughness of adults within sporting contexts have had considerable success (Gucciardi et al., 2009; Slack et al., 2015; Miçooğullari & Ekmekçi, 2017). However, there has been limited evidence in relation to the importance of mental toughness within educational settings. One case study that focused on the development of mental toughness in Year 11 pupils (aged 15–16) reported improvements in the control and confidence elements of mental toughness following the intervention (Clough et al., 2016). One of the biggest unintended consequences of this study was the impact on the teachers selected for training and delivery of the mental toughness lessons. The analysis, completed using the MTQ48, a mental toughness questionnaire, found a significant upward trend in all aspects of mental toughness and a significant increase in confidence. Teachers reported that they were using the same techniques that they were using with the pupils and that they were more self-aware of the impact of their own mental toughness after completing the mental toughness training.

An additional advantage of the mental toughness framework is that the concepts consistently correlate with wellbeing measures (Lin et al., 2017; Stamp et al., 2015). In adolescents, higher levels of mental toughness are associated with lower levels of depressive symptoms in times of high stress (Gerber et al., 2013). Psychological wellbeing (including depression and anxiety) have been found to correlate with adolescents' mental toughness, with females reporting lower levels of mental toughness and higher rates of depression and anxiety compared to males (McGeown et al., 2016). This gender difference is consistent with previous studies that found male adolescents report higher levels of mental toughness than female adolescents (St Clair-Thompson et al., 2015; Gerber et al., 2013).

What does this mean in practice?

Mental toughness is a useful framework when delivering a non-cognitive skills programme in the primary school classroom. Using a conceptual framework such as the mental toughness model to combine various approaches, such as growth mindset and grit, increases consistent use of language and ideology during sessions as well as during lessons delivered by teaching staff at other times. This study shows that both teachers and pupils reported significant differences in pupil non-cognitive skills following this relatively short intervention. Therefore, the study provides a guide for future classroom-based interventions in terms of content. We have used this study to support the development of the activities in this book, as well as our experience from other projects aimed at developing pupils' non-cognitive abilities.

However, using the mental toughness model with the inclusion of both self-report and subjective instruments provides schools with a simple framework. In this book, we have attempted to map each activity on to the development of one of the 'Cs' in the mental toughness model, rather than the vague notion of developing a 'mindset'. However, you will see that there is probably some overlap between the activities and the component of mental toughness that we were aiming to develop.

We would argue that this method makes operationalising non-cognitive skills in the primary school classroom much easier for the practitioner. The concept of mental toughness has the added benefit of already being part of young people's daily speech, which means that it may be perceived as a less academic resource than other psychology concepts (Gerber et al., 2013). Scalability of the programme is good as it meets the previously suggested criteria: it has already been successfully delivered, expectations for delivery are standardised, and resources are available to enable implementation by teachers (Dawson et al., 2018). Of course, you might want to use a combination of resources, not just the ones suggested in this book.

One issue that we've seen with all aspects of work around mindset programmes is that the interventions often seem very brief. It's very difficult from the literature to be specific about the amount of time that should be dedicated to the delivery of interventions. In this book, we've aimed for somewhere in the middle. We've found that these sessions are best delivered in shorter blocks.

The other issue is repetition. We would argue that purposeful practice is often needed to see changes in behaviour or mindset that stick. This means that we shouldn't avoid repetition of activities; in fact, we should embrace it. Some of the activities in this book could be repeated many times. We've found that often, as self-awareness starts to develop, pupils get different outcomes from an activity they've already completed.

It's also important to remember that not everything works for everybody. We've seen this many times. If you expect every pupil to like or respond positively to every activity, you are going to be disappointed. If you make a change of behaviour or mindset in a small percentage of pupils in a class, you should consider this to be a huge success.

Finally, we would argue that, if you are trying to develop the mental toughness of your pupils and you don't have a framework, it becomes incredibly difficult. It is unlikely that there will ever be a 'one size fits all' approach to developing non-cognitive skills in the classroom. Contexts and individuals will always vary between schools. However, the 4C framework provides you with a lens to look at both yourself and your pupils and then the sessions provide specific activities that can target each element of the model.

Sessions for 4–5-year-olds (Reception)

Session	Focus	Outcomes	Summary	Page
1 I am good at …	Developing confidence	To identify an area of strength	This session encourages pupils to identify something that they are good at and reflect on what makes you good at something.	18
2 Inside me	Developing control and commitment	To understand what the word 'worry' means To identify ways of dealing with our worries	This session explores how we feel when we are worried about something and how we can respond to our worries.	22
3 Trying again	Developing control and commitment	To reflect on why we should try again	Using the book *Tilda Tries Again* by Tom Percival, this session explores why we should try again with challenges.	26
4 Too small	Developing challenge and confidence	To identify strengths To suggest ways that they can encourage others	This session encourages pupils not to compare themselves to others and to identify their own strengths.	29

Sessions for 4–5-year-olds (Reception)

Session	Focus	Outcomes	Summary	Page
5 Bounce	Developing control and commitment	To explore how we can 'bounce' back from challenges To understand why we should try again	This session explores attempting to do jigsaws and failing. It encourages pupils to bounce back from mistakes and challenges.	33
6 New challenges	Developing challenge	To identify something that they find challenging	This session focuses on exploring how we feel when something is challenging and helps pupils identify something they find challenging that they want to improve.	36
7 Stickability	Developing commitment	To understand what the word 'stickability' means To practise drawing a butterfly	Using the context of drawing a butterfly, this session explores stickability (commitment) and what happens when you show commitment to a challenge.	40
8 Choices	Developing control and commitment	To identify how they would respond if faced with a challenge	Using scenarios that the pupils are familiar with, this session encourages pupils to reflect on what they should commit to and begins initial discussions about the concept of commitment and making choices.	45

Overview

These sessions introduce the concept of mental toughness in bite-size chunks. The concept is reinforced through engaging stories and visual prompts. The language of the 4Cs is explored in a range of engaging activities. Pupils are given the opportunity to experience challenging activities and to begin to reflect on how they felt when they were not initially successful. At the end, the pupils begin to identify their own challenges.

Session structure

Each session (in the Reception section) has three parts:
- Whole-class introduction
- Group activity
- Reflection time

Whole-class introduction

The session begins with a whole-class introduction to the week's focus/stimulus for mental toughness. Ideally, the initial whole-class discussion should take place at the beginning of the week as this will allow enough time for the pupils to access the continuous provision and the group activity during the rest of the week.

The introductions are designed to be short and to involve the pupils as active learners, responding to the stimulus and talking to their talk partners. This will be more effective if the pupils are familiar with working with a talk partner and are clear on how to be successful at this (see *Outstanding Formative Assessment*, Chapter 4, by Shirley Clarke, 2014).

Group activity

The group activity can be led either by the teacher or another adult. During the small-group discussions, it is useful to make brief notes and to keep examples of the pupils' thoughts and suggestions. These can then be used as part of a display to reinforce the concepts.

Reflection time

Reflection time needs to take place once the pupils have had access to the different opportunities in the classroom. Again, it is a short session, facilitated by the teacher, that brings together ideas and challenges the pupils' thinking further.

SESSIONS FOR 4–5-YEAR-OLDS (RECEPTION)

1 I am good at …

Summary

This session encourages pupils to identify something they are good at and reflect on what makes you good at something.

Focus

Developing confidence

Outcome

To identify an area of strength

Resources

Teaching slides: Reception Session 1
Handout: I am good at …
Counters

Early Learning Goals

Self-regulation

Pupils at the expected level of development will show an understanding of their own feelings and those of others, and begin to regulate their behaviour accordingly.

Managing self

Pupils at the expected level of development will be confident to try new activities and show independence, resilience and perseverance in the face of challenge.

Whole-class introduction

1. Arrange the pupils into a circle, sitting next to their talk partner.
2. Explain to the pupils that there are no right or wrong answers and that you are just interested in their opinions.
3. Pose the question:
   What does it mean if you are 'good at something'?
   Provide the pupils with some talk time and then take feedback.
4. After the pupils have shared their ideas, ensure that you clarify the meaning of what being good at something looks like.

1 I AM GOOD AT …

> **Visible Thinking** 👁
>
> **Being good at something** means that you have learnt to do it, that you have practised, made mistakes and learnt how to get better at it. Even though you are 'good' at something you may still be able to improve, e.g. if you are good at drawing you can still get better at drawing and including more detail.

5 Print out the **handout** enlarged to A3 size (or use the **teaching slide**) and place the images and the question mark in the centre of the circle of pupils. You may wish to personalise the images to reflect things that your pupils may perceive themselves to be 'good' at both at home and in school.

6 Recap briefly on what each image represents.
   - I am good at reading
   - I am good at riding a bike
   - I am good at building models
   - I am good at writing
   - I am good at playing on my device
   - Something else (represented by the question mark)

7 Explain to the pupils that you are going to identify something that you are good at.

8 Select something that you are good at and explain why you have selected it.

> **Visible Thinking** 👁
>
> I am good at drawing because I have got better and I can now draw people and include their features, such as their nose, ears and eyes.

SESSIONS FOR 4–5-YEAR-OLDS (RECEPTION)

> 9 Place a counter on the image of the thing that you are good at (remember this could be the question mark) and then provide every pupil with the opportunity to identify an area that they are good at, using the **handout**. The use of the counters allows every pupil to identify an area.
>
> 10 Review the areas that the class collectively finds challenging and explain that you will be thinking about this.

Group activity

1. Revisit the images of the things that the pupils identified themselves as being good at. Explore this question with the pupils:
   What makes you good at something?
2. Then develop the discussions further by asking the pupils:
   How do you feel when you are good at something? Why?
3. Take feedback from the pupils and then ask them to think about:
   Is it easy to be good at something?
   Why do you think that?
   During the discussions, collect the pupils' ideas on a large piece of paper or on the interactive whiteboard so they can be revisited.

Reflection time

1. Explain to the pupils that, if we are good at something, we can use this to help others.
   Ask:
   How can we help someone who is finding something challenging?
2. Revisit the pupils' ideas about what they are successful at and use them to create a display.
   I have learnt to be good at … and I can help you.

Follow up

Utilise opportunities to model the learning process and how you can improve and be 'good' at something. Use visible thinking to model the process.

1 I AM GOOD AT …

Pupils' responses

What does it mean if you are 'good at something'?

- 'You can do something by yourself.'
- 'You can do it.'
- 'It's easy.'

How do you feel when you are good at something? Why?

- 'Happy.'
- 'Pleased with myself.'
- 'Excited.'

How can we help someone who is finding something challenging?

- 'Tell them to try.'
- 'Say "You can do it."'
- 'Help them.'
- 'Tell them that they are good at something.'

Is it easy to be good at something?

- 'Some things.'
- 'Sometimes, but you have to work hard.'

2 Inside me

Summary

This session explores how we feel when we are worried about something and how we can respond to our worries.

Focus

Developing control and commitment

Outcomes

To understand what the word 'worry' means
To identify ways of dealing with our worries

Resources

Teaching slides: Reception Session 2
Handout: Outline of a child
Playdough

Early Learning Goals

Self-regulation

Pupils at the expected level of development will:

- show an understanding of their own feelings and those of others, and begin to regulate their behaviour accordingly
- set and work towards simple goals, being able to wait for what they want and control their immediate impulses when appropriate.

Managing self

Pupils at the expected level of development will be confident to try new activities and show independence, resilience and perseverance in the face of challenge.

Building relationships

Pupils at the expected level of development will show sensitivity to their own and to others' needs.

Whole-class introduction

1. Arrange the pupils so they are sitting in a circle next to their talk partner.
2. Share the word 'worry' with them and then ask them to discuss:
   What does the word 'worry' mean?
   Provide the pupils with some talk time and then take feedback.

2 INSIDE ME

3 Listen to their different ideas and respond in a neutral manner, then clarify what the word 'worry' means.

> **Visible Thinking** 👁
>
> A **worry** is something that we are scared about doing. We can have worries about doing new things or we can worry about making mistakes or something that has happened.

4 Display the **teaching slide** and explain to the pupils that the playdough is our blob of feelings and can represent the different ways we can feel.

> **Visible Thinking** 👁
>
> Explain to the pupils that we have lots of feelings inside us.

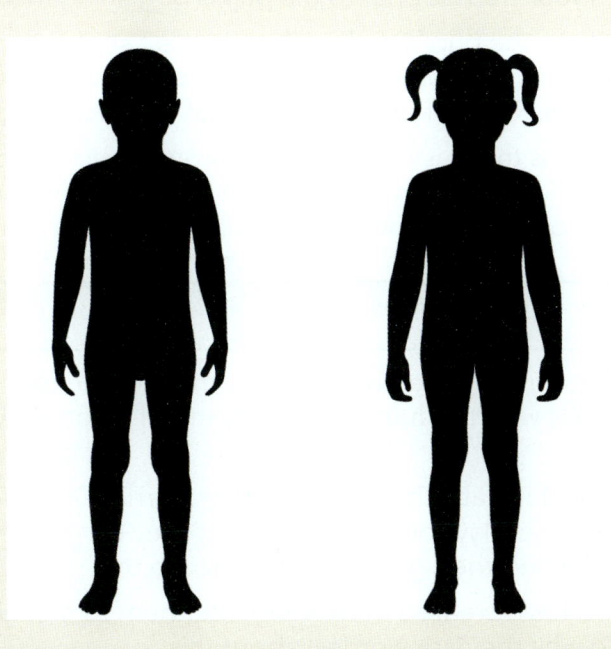

5 Remind pupils of the different emotions/feelings that they may have and ask them to show you how their face shows how they are feeling:
   Show me a sad face …
   Repeat for the different emotions. If appropriate, you may need to model for the pupils to ensure they understand the different feelings.

6 Use a piece of playdough and the **handout** to model to the pupils something that you are worried about. As you break down the worry into smaller worries, break off a piece of the playdough to represent it and put it onto the handout. Try to do this four or five times. Use a worry that the pupils can relate to and use visible thinking to explain clearly.

23

SESSIONS FOR 4–5-YEAR-OLDS (RECEPTION)

> ### Visible Thinking
>
> I am worried about joining the new swimming class. I am scared that I won't be able to do it! I am worried that I won't know anyone. I am worried that I won't be able to touch the floor in the swimming pool. I am worried that I will get cold.

7. Explain to the pupils that you want them to help you with your worry as you want to show 'stickability' and go to your swimming class. (The concept of stickability/commitment will be explored specifically in Session 7.)

8. Explain to the pupils that we can deal with our worries and there are things we can do to help us. Ask:

   What can we do to help us deal with our worries?

   Reiterate that there are no wrong or right answers and that you are interested in hearing their different ideas. Provide the pupils with some thinking time and then ask them to share their ideas. Initially, you may wish to model a strategy for helping with your worries prior to the pupils beginning their discussions.

9. Take feedback from the pupils and, as they suggest strategies that will help reduce your worries, remove one of the balls of playdough that represents an aspect of the worry. Repeat until each aspect of your worry has been removed.

10. Explain to the pupils that it is normal to have worries and that both adults and children have worries. Remind the pupils that there are things we can do to help us deal with our worries and that you will be revisiting it in a group activity.

Group activity

1. Begin by recapping the different emotions that we can feel and then provide the pupils with the **handout** and some playdough to represent their emotions.

2. Ask the pupils to think about something that worries them and to create their worry using the playdough. Explain that they can represent their worry however they like and then give them time to do this.

3. Once the pupils have created their worry, ask them to explain what it represents and why they are worried about this.

4. Select one pupil's worry to focus on and break it down into the different parts of the worry using the questions as prompts:

   What are you worried about?

   Why are you worried about …?

   What do you think will happen?

   Can you break your worry into smaller parts?

5. Together, break down the worry and then ask the pupils to think of things that can help with the worry.

6. Create a list of the different strategies that the pupils suggest.

Reflection time

Share with the pupils the different strategies that they can use when they are feeling worried, such as talking to an adult. Ask the pupils to reflect on the following:

Have you ever used one of these strategies?
When did you use it?
Did it help you?

Follow up

Create a class display of the pupils' worries and use it to reinforce the different strategies they can use to help them.

Pupils' responses

What does the word 'worry' mean?

> 'It means scared.'
>
> 'It means you're scared.'
>
> 'It means you're scared and might not be able to do something.'
>
> 'A monster in your bedroom might make you worried.'

What can we do to help us deal with our worries?

> 'Do it, then you will feel better.'
>
> 'Tell a joke to make yourself smile.'
>
> 'The more you do something the easier it gets.'
>
> 'Try it – bounce!'
>
> 'Stickability – try again. You can stick at it.'
>
> 'Friends can help.'
>
> 'Be brave.'
>
> 'Talk to someone about your worry.'

A pupil's response to 'I am worried about my dancing class as it is hard and is a long time.'

SESSIONS FOR 4–5-YEAR-OLDS (RECEPTION)

3 Trying again

Summary

Using the book *Tilda Tries Again* by Tom Percival, this session explores why we should try again with challenges.

Focus

Developing control and commitment

Outcome

To reflect on why we should try again

Resources

Teaching slides: Reception Session 3
Tilda Tries Again by Tom Percival (2021)
Visualiser
Materials for making model ladybirds
Film clip of a ladybird or other insect

Early Learning Goals

Self-regulation

Pupils at the expected level of development will:

- show an understanding of their own feelings and those of others, and begin to regulate their behaviour accordingly
- set and work towards simple goals, being able to wait for what they want and control their immediate impulses when appropriate.

Managing self

Pupils at the expected level of development will be confident to try new activities and show independence, resilience and perseverance in the face of challenge.

Building relationships

Pupils at the expected level of development will show sensitivity to their own and to others' needs.

Whole-class introduction

1. Arrange the pupils so they are sitting on the carpet with their talk partner and able to see the book. You may wish to put the book under a visualiser while you read it, as this enables the pupils to see the illustrations clearly.

2. Introduce the pupils to the book *Tilda Tries Again* by Tom Percival and read the story to page 12 when Tilda decides to give up.

3. Ask the pupils:
   Why has Tilda decided to do nothing?
   Provide the pupils with some time to think and then ask them to share their ideas with their partner.

4. Take feedback from the pupils and then explain to them that Tilda's world hasn't really turned upside down; she feels like that because she is stuck and can't do anything.

5. Continue reading the story to page 14 when Tilda sees the ladybird stuck on her back. Ask the pupils to discuss:
   What has happened to the ladybird?
   How will the ladybird feel?
   Provide the pupils with some talk time and then take feedback from them.

6. Explain to the pupils that they are going to be thinking about the ladybird when they work in their small group and then continue reading the story to the end. Ask the pupils to think about:
   What changed in the story?
   How did the ladybird help?

7. Take feedback from the pupils and reinforce the idea that, when Tilda kept trying, she was able to learn how to do new things. Explain that we all need to be more like the ladybird and keep trying when things are challenging.

Group activity

1. Recap the story with the pupils and then use the visualiser (or the **teaching slide**) to share an image of a ladybird stuck on its back. Ask the pupils to think about:
   How does the ladybird feel?

2. Ask the pupils to share their ideas and then develop their thinking further by asking them:
   Why does the ladybird keep trying?

3. Take feedback from the pupils and ask them to reflect on how they can be more like the ladybird and keep trying. Model the sentence:
   I am going to be more like the ladybird because I am going to keep trying with my writing.
   Provide the pupils with some thinking time and then ask them to share their ideas. Re-model the sentence and remind them to use it when speaking.

SESSIONS FOR 4–5-YEAR-OLDS (RECEPTION)

> ### Reflection time
> Share with the pupils the image of the ladybird on its back using the **teaching slide**. Ask them to reflect on how it is feeling and why it tries again. Provide the pupils with some talk time and then gather their ideas. Then ask some of the pupils to share what they want to keep trying at. Sharing every child's focus encourages the pupils to support and encourage each other and develops collective efficacy.

> ### Follow up
> Pupils can create their own model ladybirds for a display to reinforce the idea of trying again.
>
> Watch a short film clip of a ladybird or other insect persevering until they are back on their feet.

Pupils' responses

Why has Tilda decided to do nothing?
- ‘Because she feels like she can't do anything.’
- ‘Because she doesn't want to try and do things she can't do.’
- ‘Because she thinks she can't do something that her friends can do.’

What has happened to the ladybird?
- ‘It's upside down.’
- ‘It's stuck.’

How will the ladybird feel?
- ‘Sad.’
- ‘Scared.’
- ‘Stuck.’

What changed in the story?
- ‘Tilda thought she could try.’

How did the ladybird help?
- ‘The ladybird showed her how to try.’
- ‘She wanted to be like the ladybird.’

4 Too small

Summary

This session encourages pupils not to compare themselves to others and to identify their own strengths.

Focus

Developing challenge and confidence

Outcome

To identify strengths

To suggest ways that they can encourage others

Resources

Teaching slides: Reception Session 4

Handout: What would you say?

Early Learning Goals

Self-regulation

Pupils at the expected level of development will show an understanding of their own feelings and those of others, and begin to regulate their behaviour accordingly.

Managing self

Pupils at the expected level of development will be confident to try new activities and show independence, resilience and perseverance in the face of challenge.

Whole-class introduction

1. Arrange the pupils so they are sitting with their talk partner and can see the board.
2. Using the **first teaching slide**, share the image of the elephant and the mouse and ask the pupils to think about:
   What do you notice?
3. Provide the pupils with a few minutes to discuss their ideas with their partner. During the discussions, observe and listen to the pupils' ideas. You could record their ideas to display and to stimulate further discussions.

SESSIONS FOR 4–5-YEAR-OLDS (RECEPTION)

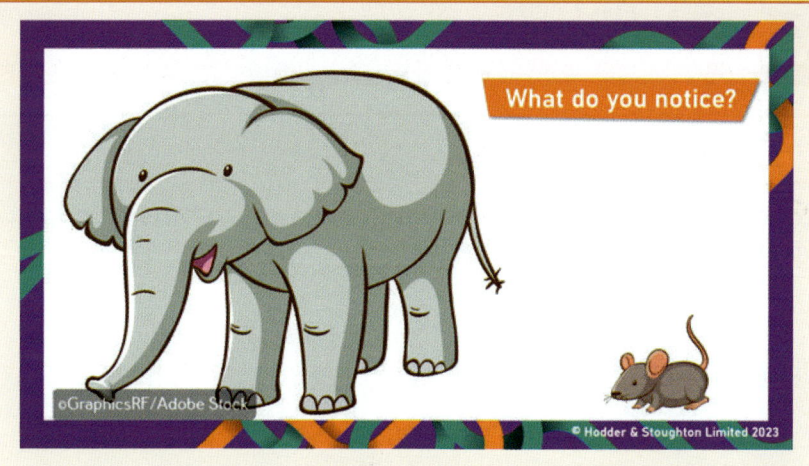

[Teaching slide: elephant and mouse with caption "What do you notice?"]

4. Once you have taken feedback from the pupils, ensure that you reinforce the idea that the animals are different.

5. Develop the pupils' thinking further by sharing the **next teaching slide** showing the elephant and the mouse where the mouse is sharing its feelings. Read how the mouse is feeling to the pupils and then read it together.

[Teaching slide: elephant and mouse with speech bubble "I am too small. I can't do anything!"]

6. Share with the pupils that the mouse is the elephant's friend to prevent the pupils focusing their thinking on the mouse feeling lonely.

7. Ask the pupils to imagine that they are the mouse and to think carefully about how the mouse is feeling when saying 'I am too small. I can't do anything!' Encourage them to think about why the mouse is saying these words and ask:

   How does the mouse feel?

8. Develop this further by asking the pupils to talk to their partner about how the mouse is feeling. Pre-empt their discussions by asking the pupils to think of three different words to describe how the mouse is feeling.

9. Ask the pupils to show you that they are ready to share their thoughts by giving a signal (e.g. placing a finger on their nose). Take feedback from them and probe their thinking further by asking:

   Why do you think the mouse feels like that?

10 Explain to the pupils that the elephant is the mouse's friend and the elephant wants to encourage the mouse to have self-belief. Ask the pupils to think about:
What could the elephant say to encourage the mouse?

11 Provide the pupils with some talk time and during their discussions eavesdrop on their conversations. Collect some of their ideas on the board.

12 Share some of the pupils' ideas and then explain that they will be thinking about this more in a small group.

Group activity

1. Revisit the image of the elephant and the mouse in which the mouse describes how it is feeling.

2. Ask the pupils to reflect on the mouse and how it is feeling. Focus the discussions by asking the pupils:
   How is the mouse feeling?
   Why does the mouse feel like that?

3. Explain to the pupils that they are going to imagine that they are the elephant and the mouse is their friend. Ask them to reflect on how they would encourage the mouse to have a go at something. You may wish to share possible scenarios that the mouse may be reluctant to try such as climbing a tree, reading a book, etc.
   What would you say to the mouse to encourage it to try?

4. Provide the pupils with some thinking time and then collect their ideas. You could scribe the pupils' ideas to share with the rest of the class later or the pupils could record their ideas independently in a follow-up writing activity, using the **handout**.

Reflection time

Share some examples of the pupils' ideas of what to say to the mouse to encourage it to try to do something. You may wish to share the written recordings of their ideas. Explore the ideas and share opportunities within the classroom when they could use the phrases to encourage their friends to try.

Follow up

Ask the pupils to reflect on their own personal experience. Ask them:
Have you ever felt like the mouse?
Collect examples of the scenarios and use them to create a display along with the pupils' ideas of what to say to someone who feels this way.

SESSIONS FOR 4–5-YEAR-OLDS (RECEPTION)

Pupils' responses

What do you notice?
'A mouse with a short tail and an elephant with a long tail.'
'One has a large nose. They are different.'
'One has big ears and one has small ears.'
'It is easier to see the elephant than the mouse because it's big.'

How does the mouse feel?
'Lonely – he wants some friends.'
'Sad.'
'Small – too small.'
'Unhappy because he can't do it.'
'Cross – as he is too small and can't do anything.'

What would you say to the mouse to encourage him to try?
'I could help you.'
'Cheer up! You are good at running.'
'You can do it.'
'Keep trying!'
'Just try again!'

Have you ever felt like the mouse?
'When I couldn't do a forward roll.'
'When I couldn't reach up high for something.'
'When I found it hard to concentrate.'

What would you say?

Try, try, try
You can jump high!
I can help you.

A pupil's response to 'What could the elephant say to the mouse?'

5 Bounce

Summary

This session explores attempting to do jigsaws and failing. It encourages pupils to bounce back from mistakes and challenges.

Focus

Developing control and commitment

Outcomes

To explore how we can 'bounce' back from challenges
To understand why we should try again

Resources

Teaching slides: Reception Session 5

Jigsaw puzzles of various levels of challenge but on a similar theme (and one that is partially completed)

Ball that bounces

Tweezers

Early Learning Goals

Self-regulation

Pupils at the expected level of development will:

- show an understanding of their own feelings and those of others, and begin to regulate their behaviour accordingly
- set and work towards simple goals, being able to wait for what they want and control their immediate impulses when appropriate.

Managing self

Pupils at the expected level of development will be confident to try new activities and show independence, resilience and perseverance in the face of challenge.

Building relationships

Pupils at the expected level of development will show sensitivity to their own and to others' needs.

Sessions for 4–5-year-olds (Reception)

Whole-class introduction

1. Arrange the pupils so they are sitting in a circle and are able to see you clearly.
2. Place the partially completed jigsaw in the centre of the circle and silently model trying to put the missing pieces in. Modelling silently reduces cognitive load and enables the pupils to focus on your behaviour and responses.
3. Model trying but failing to put the missing pieces into the jigsaw. Repeat this and slowly begin to show your frustration through your facial expressions and physical response. Continue demonstrating the behaviours until you reach the point of giving up.
4. Ask the pupils to reflect on:
   How am I feeling? Why?
   What am I trying to do?
   Why am I getting it wrong?
   Select some pupils to respond and share their ideas. As you listen to their responses and provide feedback, ensure that you do so in a neutral voice. This will encourage the pupils to share ideas openly.
5. Develop the pupils' thinking further by asking them:
   Do you think I want to try again? Why?
   Provide the pupils with some thinking time and then gather feedback from them. Again, respond in a neutral voice to encourage the pupils to share their ideas.
6. Then encourage the pupils to reflect on how they would feel in the same situation. Ask them to think about:
   If you were me and trying to do the jigsaw, would you try again?
   Ask the pupils to indicate their response by a show of hands and then probe their thinking further:
   Why would you try again?
   Why don't you want to try again?
7. Silently, model bouncing a ball in front of the pupils. You could also display the **teaching slide**. Repeat this activity and then ask the pupils:
   What happens to the ball when I drop it?
8. Take feedback from the pupils and then explain to them:

Visible Thinking

When we find things challenging or we are stuck, we need to be able to bounce like the ball did. We need to get back up and try again, and not worry if we have made a mistake.

9. Then model attempting to do the jigsaw again and this time, after a few attempts, being successful. When modelling, ensure you share your feelings with the pupils, e.g:

This is tricky, I will try putting the piece in this way. That didn't work. I will try this way. When I turn it this way, it fits! I am glad I kept trying.

Group activity

1. Share with the pupils a range of jigsaws of different levels of challenge. Ensure they are all on a similar theme and there isn't one that the pupils would prefer due to the characters it contains. Ask the pupils:
   Which is the easiest jigsaw? Why?
   Take feedback from the pupils and encourage them to share what makes the jigsaw easier.

2. Develop the pupils' thinking further by asking them:
   Which jigsaws are more challenging? Why?
   Ask the pupils for some feedback and then together sort the jigsaws into an order from the easiest to the hardest.

3. Provide the pupils with some time to attempt to complete the jigsaws and encourage them to persevere and stick at the activity.

Reflection time

Bounce the ball again and remind the pupils about the importance of bouncing back up and sticking with challenging activities. Share examples of when you have observed the pupils bouncing during their learning this week.

Follow up

Provide the pupils with the opportunity to explore different levels of challenge in their activities, e.g. the jigsaws, a range of activities for fine motor skills, such as using tweezers to move a range of objects.

Regularly share examples of when a pupil has bounced. These could be shared as displays on a board. Ensure there is an opportunity for every pupil to share how they have bounced.

Pupils' responses

How am I feeling? Why?
- 'Sad.'
- 'Fed up!'
- 'Not feeling great because you can't do it.'
- 'Angry with yourself because you can't do it.'
- 'Annoyed.'

What am I trying to do?
- 'Make the jigsaw.'

Why am I getting it wrong?
- 'Because you are getting fed up.'
- 'Because you are being grumpy.'
- 'You are putting them in upside down.'

SESSIONS FOR 4–5-YEAR-OLDS (RECEPTION)

6 New challenges

Summary

This session focuses on exploring how we feel when something is challenging and helps pupils identify something they find challenging that they want to improve.

Focus

Developing challenge

Outcomes

To identify something that they find challenging

Resources

Teaching slides: Reception Session 6
Handout: Potential challenges
Counters

Early Learning Goals

Self-regulation

Pupils at the expected level of development will:
- show an understanding of their own feelings and those of others, and begin to regulate their behaviour accordingly
- set and work towards simple goals, being able to wait for what they want and control their immediate impulses when appropriate.

Managing self

Pupils at the expected level of development will be confident to try new activities and show independence, resilience and perseverance in the face of challenge.

Building relationships

Pupils at the expected level of development will show sensitivity to their own and to others' needs.

Whole-class introduction

1. Arrange the pupils into a circle, sitting alongside their talk partner.
2. Pose the question:

   What does the word 'challenge' mean?

   Explain to the pupils that there are no right or wrong answers and that you are just interested in their opinions. Provide the pupils with some talk time and then take feedback.

6 NEW CHALLENGES

3. After the pupils have shared their ideas, ensure that you clarify the meaning of challenge.

Visible Thinking

A **challenge** is not about what others do. Instead, it is something that is hard, that you might not be able to do and that you want to learn to do.

4. Print out the **handout** enlarged to A3 size (or use the **teaching slide**) and place the images and the question mark in the centre of the circle of pupils. You may wish to personalise the images to reflect things that your pupils find challenging both at home and in school. Briefly go over what each image represents.

Potential challenges

© Hodder & Stoughton Limited 2023

5. Explain to the pupils that you are going to identify something that you find challenging and want to get better at. Sharing the fact that you find things challenging normalises the experience. Model selecting your challenge and explaining why you have selected it.

Visible Thinking

I find learning to write great stories challenging because I find it tricky to think of ideas.

6. Place a counter on the image of the thing that you find challenging and then, using the **handouts**, provide every pupil with the opportunity to identify something that they find challenging. The use of the counters allows every pupil to identify something.

7. Review the things that the class collectively finds challenging and explain that you will be thinking about this.

SESSIONS FOR 4–5-YEAR-OLDS (RECEPTION)

Group activity

1. Revisit the images of the different things that the pupils found challenging. Explore with the pupils:
   Which do you find challenging? Why?
2. Then develop the discussions further by asking the pupils:
   How do you feel when something is challenging? Why?
3. Take feedback from the pupils and then ask them to think about:
   How can we help someone who is finding something challenging?
   What could we say?
   What could we do?
4. You may wish to model some practical strategies or things the pupils could say to encourage their thinking, e.g:
   You could say 'It's okay'.
   You could tell them to try again.
   Collect the pupils' ideas on a large piece of paper or on the interactive whiteboard so they can be revisited.

Reflection time

Revisit the pupils' ideas about how they can all respond when something is challenging. Reinforce the idea of encouraging each other to try new challenges. Explain that you have set up a number of challenges around the classroom for them to try, e.g:
- images of tricky patterns for them to create
- very small objects that must be moved by tweezers.

Follow up

Have a symbol that you use in the classroom to identify that something is challenging, e.g. some new learning or a specific activity. Pre-empting that something will be tricky helps to support the pupils to rise to new challenges and ensures they become more comfortable with the concept.

You could choose an image of a mountain or steps to success to represent a challenge.

Share the symbol with parents so that they can use it at home and help the pupils to become more comfortable with the idea of challenging themselves.

Pupils' responses

What does the word 'challenge' mean?

> 'When it is hard to do something.'

> 'A challenge could be to win a race.'

> 'One time, I couldn't do a backwards roll. That's a challenge.'

> 'Skipping can be a challenge – as I can't do it.'

How do you feel when something is challenging? Why?

> 'I feel small.'

> 'Sad and angry because I can't do it.'

> 'A bit grumpy – because I think I can't do it, but I keep on trying.'

> 'Nervous.'

How can we help someone who is finding something challenging?

> 'Tell them to try.'

> 'Say "You can do it".'

> 'Help them.'

> 'Tell them that they are good at something.'

SESSIONS FOR 4–5-YEAR-OLDS (RECEPTION)

7 Stickability

Summary

Using the context of drawing a butterfly, this session explores stickability (commitment) and what happens when you show commitment to a challenge.

Focus

Developing commitment

Outcomes

To understand what the word 'stickability' means
To practise drawing a butterfly

Resources

Teaching slides: Reception Session 7
Handout: Stickability

Early Learning Goals

Self-regulation

Pupils at the expected level of development will:

- show an understanding of their own feelings and those of others, and begin to regulate their behaviour accordingly
- set and work towards simple goals, being able to wait for what they want and control their immediate impulses when appropriate.

Managing self

Pupils at the expected level of development will be confident to try new activities and show independence, resilience and perseverance in the face of challenge.

Whole-class introduction

1. Arrange the pupils so they can see the image of the butterfly clearly on the **teaching slide**.

   Ask the pupils to look closely at the image and think about:

   What can you see?

   What do you notice?

   Provide the pupils with some thinking time and then take feedback from them.

2. Explain to the pupils that you are going to try to draw the butterfly. Silently model attempting to draw the butterfly and becoming frustrated with your attempts.

> ### 👁 Visible Thinking
> Explain what you are trying to do and the mistakes that you are making. Explain to the pupils how you are feeling and what you think of your attempt at drawing the butterfly.

3. Ask the pupils to think about:
   Why am I feeling frustrated?
   Take feedback from the pupils.

4. Explain to the pupils that you want to 'bounce' and try again with your drawing of a butterfly. Distribute the **handouts**, which contain four boxes for four different attempts.

5. Explain to the pupils that they need to look closely at what you are going to do and listen very carefully.

6. Model drawing the butterfly again in the first box. As you are drawing it, look closely at the image of the butterfly and describe what you are drawing.

7. Once you have finished your first attempt, pause and ask the pupils to look closely at your drawing. Ask them to think about:
   What is good about my drawing?
   How can I make it better?
   Take feedback from the pupils.

8. Explain to the pupils that you are going to show 'stickability' (commitment) and try again. Model to the pupils your second attempt at drawing the butterfly (in the second box on the handout).

> ### 👁 Visible Thinking
> Explain to the pupils what you are drawing and how you have listened to their feedback and are now including the antennae, etc.

9. Once you have finished your second attempt, again ask the pupils to look closely at your drawing. Ask them to think about:
   What is good about my drawing?
   How can I make it better?
   Take feedback from the pupils.

10. Explain to the pupils that you are going to try again and show even more stickability. Model to the pupils your third attempt at drawing the butterfly.

Sessions for 4–5-year-olds (Reception)

> ### 👁 Visible Thinking
>
> Explain to the pupils what you are drawing and how you have listened to their feedback and are now including the patterns on the wings, etc.

11 Once you have finished your third attempt, again ask the pupils to look closely at your drawing. Ask them to think about:

What is good about my drawing?

How can I make it better?

Take feedback from the pupils.

12 Explain to the pupils that you are going to show 'stickability' (commitment) and try again. Model to the pupils your fourth attempt at drawing the butterfly.

> ### 👁 Visible Thinking
>
> Explain to the pupils what you are drawing and how you have listened to their feedback and are now including the shading, etc.

13 Once you have finished your drawing, ask the pupils to review all four of your attempts. Ask them to think about:

Which is the most successful? Why?

Take feedback from the pupils.

14 Develop their thinking further by asking them:

How did I show stickability?

Group activity

1 Explain to the pupils that they are going to show 'stickability' and attempt to draw the butterfly. Provide them with an image of the butterfly to examine and then ask them to attempt to draw the butterfly.

2 Once the pupils have attempted their first try, review their drawings. Provide feedback on where they have been successful and then identify how they can improve their drawing. Model using the phrase 'I challenge you to …'. The process of highlighting where they have been successful and then providing feedback on their next steps encourages pupils to have 'stickability' and a desire to improve.

3 Then provide the pupils with time to attempt the drawings again. Once they have completed them, ask them to look carefully at their drawing and the image of the butterfly. Ask them to reflect on:

What is successful in your drawing?

How can you challenge yourself to improve it further?

Repeat these steps until the pupils have demonstrated stickability. Then ask them to identify which of their drawings they think is most successful and why.

7 STICKABILITY

> **Reflection time**
>
> Share with the pupils an example of the pupils' stickability and then ask them to describe the different attempts and how they have improved to their partner.

> **Visible Thinking** 👁
>
> In the first attempt, you have included the wings and the body. In the second attempt, you have included more detail and the patterns on the wings. In the third attempt, you have made the body smaller which is the same as on the photograph. In your final attempt, there is great detail on the wings, the shape of the wings is good and the body is the same as in the photograph.

> **Follow up**
>
> The stickability activity could be used across the curriculum and in all the different year groups, e.g. showing stickability when spelling words or solving problems in maths.

Pupils' responses

What can you see?
- 'A butterfly.'

What do you notice?
- 'It's got wings.'
- 'It has white dots over the orange part.'
- 'It's flying.'
- 'It has two antennae.'
- 'It looks like it has a tail.'

Why I am feeling frustrated?
- 'Because your picture doesn't look like the butterfly.'
- 'It looks like a flower not a butterfly.'

Pupils' feedback

What is good about my drawing?
- 'Your wings are the same as in the photograph.'
- 'It's the same shape.'

How can I make it better?
- 'It would be even better if you put the antennae on.'
- 'It would be even better if you remembered the dots.'

SESSIONS FOR 4–5-YEAR-OLDS (RECEPTION)

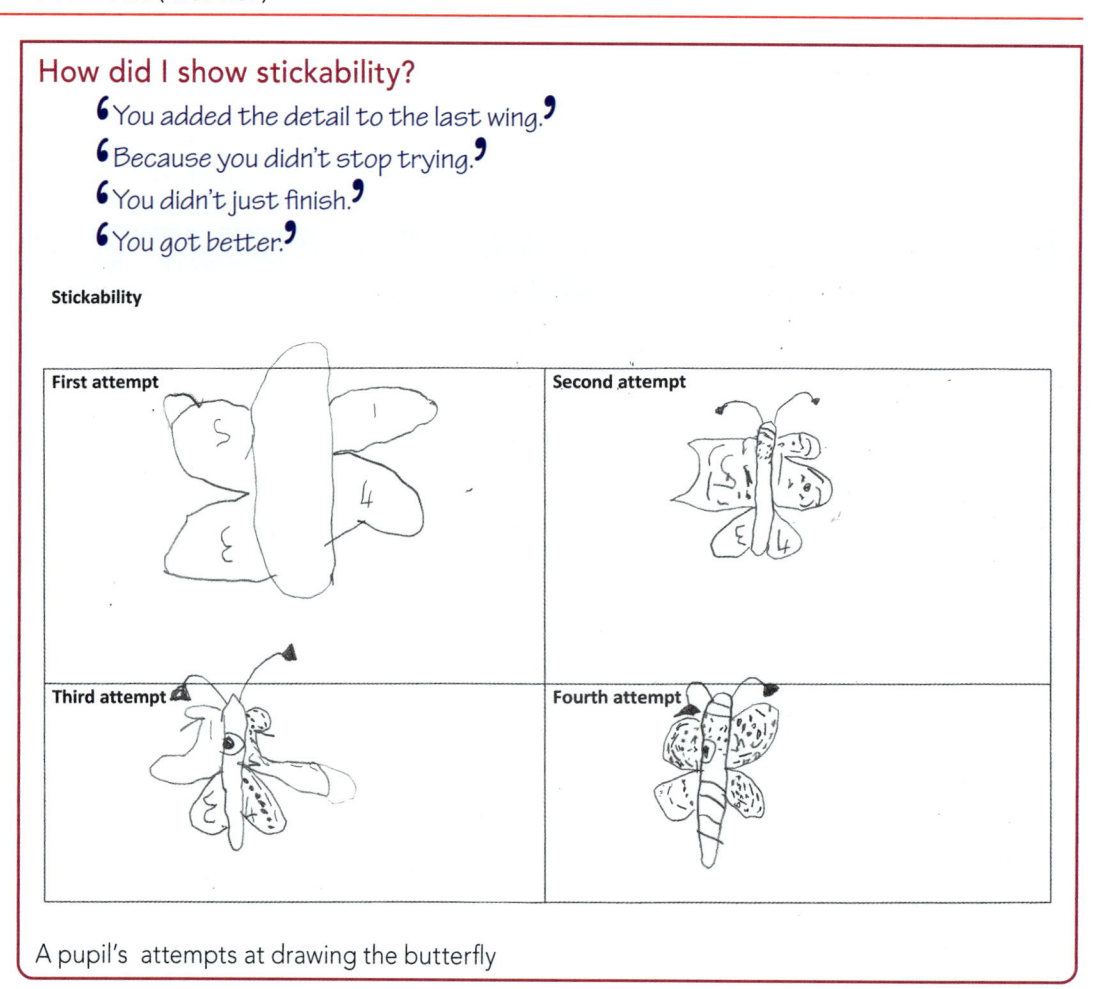

How did I show stickability?

'You added the detail to the last wing.'

'Because you didn't stop trying.'

'You didn't just finish.'

'You got better.'

Stickability

First attempt	Second attempt
Third attempt	Fourth attempt

A pupil's attempts at drawing the butterfly

8 Choices

Summary

Using scenarios that the pupils are familiar with, this session encourages pupils to reflect on what they should commit to and begins initial discussions about the concept of commitment and making choices.

Focus

Developing control and commitment

Outcomes

To identify how they would respond if faced with a challenge

Resources

Teaching slides: Reception Session 8
Handout: Different responses activity cards

Early Learning Goals

Managing self

Pupils at the expected level of development will:

- be confident to try new activities and show independence, resilience and perseverance in the face of challenge
- set and work towards simple goals, being able to wait for what they want and control their immediate impulses when appropriate.

Self-regulation

Pupils at the expected level of development will show an understanding of their own feelings and those of others, and begin to regulate their behaviour accordingly.

Whole-class introduction

1. Arrange the pupils so they are sitting with their talk partner and can see the board. Have the handout of activity cards ready for the pupils to access.
2. Explain to the pupils that an adult wants them to come and read their book to practise their reading. Display the **first teaching slide** showing the different images of potential things that they could do when asked to read. Explain to the pupils what each image represents.

[Image: four-panel graphic with labels "Read their book", "Say no", "Play with their toys", "Hide"]

3. Give the pupils the **handouts** and explain to them that there are no right or wrong answers. Ask them:

   What would you choose to do if asked to read?

   Provide the pupils with some thinking time.

4. Ask the pupils to indicate which response they would give to being asked to practise their reading. The pupils can respond by raising their hands or giving a thumbs-up to indicate what they would do.

5. Review the pupils' responses and probe their thinking further by asking:

   Why did you choose to do this?

   Is reading easy?

6. Ask the pupils to reflect on:

   Why do you think that some people would want to hide rather than read?

   Which would be the best choice to make? Why?

   Explain to the pupils that there are no right or wrong answers and that you are just interested in their opinions. Provide the pupils with some talk time and then ask them to share their ideas.

7. Remind the pupils about the positives of choosing to practise their reading, including how this will help them improve, that they will be learning, that they will be able to ask for help and that, once they have practised, they can do other things.

8 Choices

Group activity

1. Explain to the pupils that they have been asked to join a new class to learn how to swim, where they don't know anybody, and it is going to be tricky. Ask the pupils to reflect on how they might feel. Create a list of the different emotions that they may be feeling and then explain to them that doing something new can be challenging for us.

2. Display the **next teaching slide** and share with the pupils the different images of how they could respond to going swimming. Clearly explain what each image represents.

3. Then ask them to think about how they would respond and why they would respond in that way. Review the pupils' responses and probe their thinking further by asking:

   Why did you choose to do this?

4. Ask the pupils to reflect on:

   Which would be the best choice to make? Why?

   Explain to the pupils that there are no right or wrong answers and that you are just interested in their opinions. Provide the pupils with some talk time and then ask them to share their ideas.

Reflection time

Revisit the different scenarios and ask the pupils:

How did you respond at first?

Would you have changed how you responded?

SESSIONS FOR 4–5-YEAR-OLDS (RECEPTION)

> **Follow up**
>
> Display the **handouts** in the classroom as visual prompts to encourage the pupils to try.

Pupils' responses

What would you choose to do if asked to read?

Why did you choose to do this?

> 'Read – as I want to get better.'
>
> 'Reading – so I can challenge myself.'
>
> 'Say no – because it's hard.'
>
> 'Say no – because I don't want to.'
>
> 'Play with building blocks – as I like building.'
>
> 'Play with building blocks – I like building with my friends.'
>
> 'Hide – because I am scared.'

Which would be the best choice to make? Why?

> 'Reading – because you will get better.'
>
> 'Reading – you need to practise your reading.'
>
> 'Reading – you need to keep trying.'

Would you have changed how you responded?

> 'No, because you are fed up.'
>
> 'No, because it is too hard.'

Sessions for 5–6-year-olds (Year 1)

Session title	Focus	Outcome	Summary	Page
1 Wall of strength	Developing control and confidence	To reflect on how we can overcome challenges and become more confident	This session encourages pupils to reflect on how they build firm foundations and strategies for overcoming challenges. It uses a familiar context and images of a traditional tale, 'The Three Little Pigs', to spark discussions.	51
2 I can't do it!	Developing control and confidence	To reflect on how we feel when we can't do something	This session encourages pupils to reflect on how they feel when they can't do something, such as tying their shoelaces.	54
3 Giant steps	Developing challenge and commitment	To identify the small steps we should take to rise to new challenges. To sort and order the small steps that help us to learn how to tie our shoelaces	This session encourages pupils to reflect on how they can break down challenges into smaller manageable steps. It encourages them to develop commitment and rise to new challenges.	57

Sessions for 5–6-year-olds (Year 1)

Session title	Focus	Outcome	Summary	Page
4 Stickability	Developing commitment	To identify behaviours that demonstrate commitment	This session encourages pupils to reflect on how we behave when we are committed to achieving something.	60
5 Being great	Developing commitment and confidence	To identify how someone (a character) is successful To identify characteristics that make them successful	Using the book *The Littlest Yak* by Lu Fraser, this session encourages pupils to reflect on how a character is successful and to identify characteristics that contribute to their success.	63
6 Words, words, words	Developing control and confidence	To identify how certain words make us feel To suggest other phrases that we should use to give feedback	This session encourages pupils to reflect on what we say to ourselves and others, our inner voice and how we can reframe our feedback.	65
7 Power of mistakes	Developing challenge and commitment	To identify what we can learn from a mistake To develop strategies to enable us to develop when we make a mistake	This session encourages pupils to reflect on how to respond when we make a mistake and how to use the mistakes to help us grow and learn. It uses the context of maths and number bonds to 10.	68
8 My 4Cs	Developing control, challenge, commitment and confidence	To reflect and identify areas of strength To identify next steps and how to respond to challenges	This session encourages pupils to reflect on the different aspects of mental toughness and create a profile of themselves.	71

Overview

From Year 1 onwards the pupils will explicitly explore the 4Cs in familiar contexts and with real-life examples. The sessions explore how we can change our behaviours and responses to develop our mental strength. Pupils will have the opportunity to practise using different strategies which are explicitly modelled by the teacher.

1 Wall of strength

Summary

This session encourages pupils to reflect on how they build firm foundations and strategies for overcoming challenges. It uses a familiar context and images of a traditional tale, 'The Three Little Pigs', to spark discussions. Pupils need to be familiar with the story of 'The Three Little Pigs' prior to this session. A class display can be created to reinforce the discussions.

Focus

Developing control and confidence

Outcome

To reflect on how we can overcome challenges and become more confident

Resources

Teaching slides: Year 1 Session 1

Session

1. Arrange the pupils so they are sitting with a talk partner and can see the **first teaching slide** showing the 'The Three Little Pigs' houses. Explain that you are going to be exploring 'the wall of strength' with them.
   Ask the pupils:
   Do you recognise them?
   Who do they belong to?

2. Ask the pupils to think about and discuss with their talk partner:
   Which of the houses is the strongest?
   What makes it stronger than the others?
   Take feedback from the pupils and probe their ideas further by asking them to justify why it is the strongest and what they think being strong means.

3. Reveal the picture of the Big Bad Wolf on the **next teaching slide**. Ask the pupils if they recognise the character and to tell you who they think it is.
   Ask the pupils to reflect on:
   What does the wolf do in the story?
   Take feedback on the pupils' ideas and then explain that the Big Bad Wolf wanted to blow down the houses belonging to the Three Little Pigs.

SESSIONS FOR 5–6-YEAR-OLDS (YEAR 1)

4 Share the image of the Three Little Pigs again using the **next teaching slide**. Ask the pupils to think about and then discuss with their talk partner:

How do the pigs overcome the problem with the wolf?

What do they do?

Once the discussions are under way, you may wish to develop them further by asking:

What skills do they use?

5 Explain to the pupils that it can be challenging to stay strong and be resilient when we have problems like the Three Little Pigs had. Explain that being resilient means that we pick ourselves back up when things go wrong and that we know things can get better if we try to do things differently, believe in ourselves or work together.

6 Share with the pupils the image of a wall using the **next teaching slide**. Explain to the pupils that you want them to think about the things that help them to be resilient and stronger just like the wall. Ask:

How can we build our resilience?

If the pupils need further support to generate ideas, provide some suggestions, such as working with other people or taking your time. Then together create a wall containing ideas on how to overcome challenges.

Follow up

The wall of the pupils' ideas could be displayed in the classroom and used as a reference point to reinforce when pupils are displaying the characteristics of resilience.

1 WALL OF STRENGTH

Pupils' responses

Which of the houses is the strongest?
What makes it stronger than the others?

'The wall is stronger because the bricks and cement work together.'

'The cement is like glue, so it makes the wall strong, so the house made out of bricks is stronger.'

How can we build our resilience?

'Believe in yourself.'

'Ask people for help.'

'You need to keep trying and not give up.'

'Try first.'

'Stay calm.'

'Work with others.'

'Count to 10!'

'Persevere.'

'Share ideas.'

'Try your hardest.'

'Don't worry about getting it wrong.'

'Don't worry about making mistakes.'

'Be brave!'

'Practise.'

'Keep focused!'

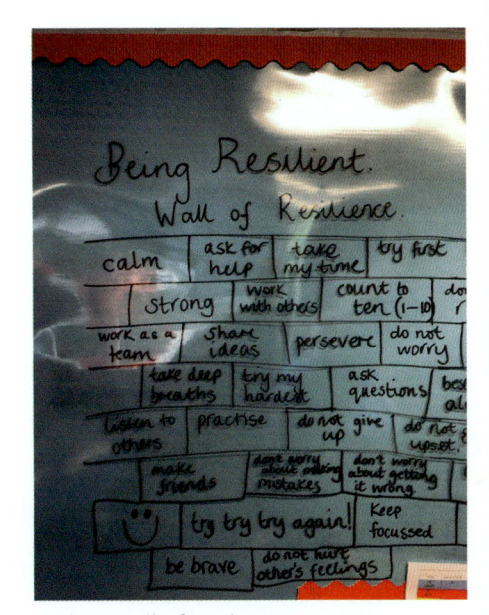

A class wall of resilience

My Wall of Strength   Name Katie

A pupil's response to 'My Wall of Strength'

53

SESSIONS FOR 5–6-YEAR-OLDS (YEAR 1)

2 I can't do it!

Summary

This session encourages pupils to reflect on how they feel when they can't do something, such as tying their shoelaces.

Focus

Developing control and confidence

Outcome

To reflect on how we feel when we can't do something

Resources

Shoe with laces
Image of teacher failing to do something (e.g. tying their shoelaces)
Image of teacher doing something successfully (e.g. tying their shoelaces)
Visualiser

Session

1. Explain to the pupils that they need to watch and listen carefully to what you are doing. Using a visualiser, model attempting to tie a shoelace. Initially model attempting to do this silently and showing your frustration that you are unable to be successful. The silent modelling will engage the pupils and allow them to process what you are trying to do. When modelling your frustration, you could stamp your feet, clench your fist, sigh, bang the shoe and demonstrate frustrated facial expressions.

2. Continue modelling your frustration and attempting to tie your shoelace. Begin to develop this further by sharing your frustration by making sounds and stating, 'I can't do it', 'It's too hard!'.

3. Ask the pupils to discuss:
   What is my problem?
   Provide the pupils with some time to discuss and eavesdrop on their conversations. Then take feedback on their discussions.

4. Develop their discussions further by posing the question:
   How did I feel when I couldn't tie my shoelace?
   When the pupils provide feedback on their ideas, probe their thinking further by asking them:
   Why do you think that?

5. Continue to develop the discussions by asking the pupils:
   How did I behave?
   Can you show me?
   The pupils can demonstrate how you behaved in conjunction with describing it as this will help reinforce the concept further.

6. While the discussions are underway you could collect the pupils' ideas on the board around an image of you trying to tie your shoelaces and being frustrated. Record how they think you feel and how you would behave. Record the pupils' ideas in two colours – one to show frustration and another to indicate positive developments, e.g. red and green.

7. Introduce the word 'frustrated' and explain that this is how we often feel when we can't do something. It can feel as if we are angry inside because we are not able to do something that we are trying to, e.g. tie our shoelaces, solve a question in maths or sound out a word accurately. Include the word 'frustrated' on the pupils' ideas board.

8. Using the visualiser, model being successful at tying your shoelaces. Initially model being successful silently and show your feelings through your facial expression and movement. Then begin to add language such as 'I did it!' and 'I have learnt how to tie my shoelaces'.
   Ask the pupils to discuss:
   How did I feel when I could tie my shoelaces?
   How did I behave?

9. Compare and contrast by reviewing the different ways you feel and behave when you can and can't do something. You may wish to use the images and pupils' ideas and display these in the classroom as visual prompts. To enable all pupils to access them, read through each word carefully and then pose the question:
   What do you notice?
   Ask the pupils to discuss this with their talk partner and then randomly select pupils to share their ideas with everyone.

Follow up

The context of this lesson could be adapted to an aspect of learning the pupils have been finding challenging.

The concept of being frustrated could form part of a class discussion during which the pupils could be asked to share when they have felt frustrated and how they coped with feeling like that.

Pupils' responses

What is my problem?

'You don't know how to tie your shoelaces.'

'You're angry.'

'You're not concentrating.'

'You're giving up!'

'You're not taking your time.'

'You're not doing it properly.'

'You don't know how to tie the shoelaces, that's the problem.'

How did I feel when I couldn't tie my shoelaces?

'Angry that you couldn't tie your shoelaces.'

'You gave up!'

'You were getting sad because you couldn't tie your shoelaces.'

'Stressed! You looked stressed.'

How did I behave?

'You messed around with the shoelaces.'

'You banged your feet because you were cross.'

'Stamped on things.'

3 Giant steps

Summary

This session encourages pupils to reflect on how they can break down challenges into smaller manageable steps. It encourages them to develop commitment and rise to new challenges.

Focus

Developing challenge and commitment

Outcome

To identify the small steps we should take to rise to new challenges
To sort and order the small steps that help us to learn how to tie our shoelaces

Resources

Teaching slides: Year 1 Session 3
Handout: Can you sequence the steps?
A shoe with shoelaces
Visualiser

Session

1. Arrange the pupils so they are sitting with a partner and able to see you clearly. Using the **first teaching slide**, share with pupils an image of a child trying to tie their shoelaces. Revisit the pupils' ideas on how you behave when you can't do something compared with how you feel when you can. Ask the pupils:

   What was I trying to do in the last session?
   What happened?

SESSIONS FOR 5–6-YEAR-OLDS (YEAR 1)

2. Revisit the word 'frustrated'. Ask the pupils to discuss with their talk partner:
   What does the word 'frustrated' mean?
   How did you know I was feeling frustrated?
   Provide the pupils with some time to discuss their ideas and then take feedback from them.

3. Model tying your shoelaces for the class and ask the pupils to reflect on:
   What did I need to know to be able to tie my shoelaces?
   Initially provide the pupils with some thinking time and then ask them to share their ideas with a partner. Eavesdrop on the conversation and gather their ideas on the board.
   You may need to model the process of tying your shoelaces to provide visual prompts for any pupil who is finding it challenging to identify the steps involved.

4. Using the **next teaching slide**, explain to the pupils that we need to break down challenges into smaller manageable steps that we can achieve.

5. Provide the pupils with the cut-out steps of learning how to tie your shoelaces from the **handout**. Read the steps to the pupils, then read them through together and finally ask the pupils to read the steps independently. This will help all of the pupils to be clear on each of the steps. You must ensure, however, that this is done in an incorrect order!

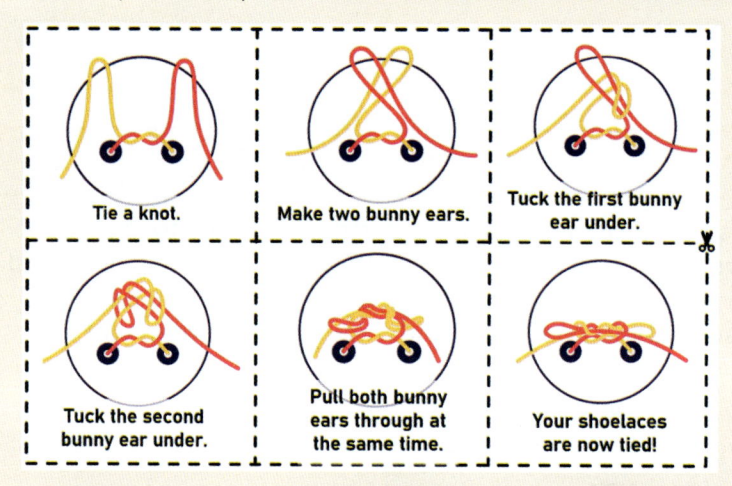

| Tie a knot. | Make two bunny ears. | Tuck the first bunny ear under. |
| Tuck the second bunny ear under. | Pull both bunny ears through at the same time. | Your shoelaces are now tied! |

6. Ask the pupils to work with a partner to organise the small steps in order to achieve the giant step of learning to tie their shoelaces. Remind the pupils that they need to think about the best order for themselves as you are interested in their ideas.

7. Share an example of how the pupils have organised the steps successfully. Ask them to explain:
   Why did you organise these steps in this order?
   If pupils need further support in understanding how to organise the steps, you could model the process of putting your shoe on, learning to tie a knot and then learning to tie your shoelaces. You could use a visualiser to show this.

3 Giant steps

> **Follow up**
>
> This same process of breaking something down and then sharing the steps could be used across the curriculum to learn something new. Pupils could also identify missing steps in the learning or steps that weren't relevant, e.g. 'cleaning your shoe'.

> **Pupils' responses**
>
> ### What did I need to know to be able to tie my shoelaces?
>
> The pupils responded in two different ways, in terms of what knowledge you would need and what learning skills you would require.
>
> **Knowledge**
> - 'How to tie a knot.'
> - 'How to thread things through.'
> - 'How to make bunny ears.'
>
> **Skills**
> - 'Concentrating.'
> - 'Watching it carefully.'
> - 'How to listen so you learn.'
>
> ### Why did you organise these steps in this order?
> - 'Because it is the right order.'
> - 'You need to do them in this order to be successful.'

SESSIONS FOR 5–6-YEAR-OLDS (YEAR 1)

4 Stickability

Summary

This session encourages pupils to reflect on how we behave when we are committed to achieving something.

Focus

Developing commitment

Outcome

To identify behaviours that demonstrate commitment

Resources

Teaching slides: Year 1 Session 4

Session

1. Arrange the pupils so they are sitting with a talk partner and can see the board clearly. Using the **first teaching slide**, share with the pupils the images of glue, sticky putty and sticky tape and ask them to reflect on:
   How are these connected?
   Explain to the pupils that there are no right or wrong answers and that you are interested in hearing their different opinions. Provide the pupils with some time to discuss their ideas with a partner. Take feedback from the pupils.

4 Stickability

2. Share with the pupils the image of the glue stick (labelled with the word 'stickability'). Explain to the pupils that stickability means not giving up, sticking at something even though it may be hard and challenging to do so.

3. Explain that another word for 'stickability' is commitment, that being committed and showing stickability are the same. Reinforce this concept further by explaining that, when we show commitment or 'stickability', we have an invisible glue that helps us to stick at things which we find challenging and tricky.

4. You may wish to share a personal experience where you have shown stickability, as this will help reinforce the concept with the pupils, e.g. learning to drive a car when you did not pass your test on the first attempt.

5. Explain to the pupils that they are going to be detectives and that they are going to be looking for ways in which people have demonstrated stickability.

6. Using the **next two teaching slides**, share on the board scenarios that demonstrate different ways in which pupils have reacted to challenging tasks. Take each one in turn and read it together, then ask the pupils to think about it and discuss it with their partner:

    Does this demonstrate 'stickability'?

    Arthur's mum wants him to read his reading book but he finds it tricky so he is refusing to read with her. Does Arthur have stickability?

    Jenna has been trying to draw a house. She listened carefully to the teacher and has been practising. She tries to practise every day to help her get better. Does Jenna have stickability?

7. Initially, the pupils should respond with a show of hands as to whether the child is demonstrating stickability. Pupils should then be probed further on this by asking:

    Why do you think that?

    How are they showing stickability?

8. Select one of the scenarios where the child is not demonstrating stickability and ask the pupils to reflect on:

    What does … need to do to show stickability?

Follow up

A display could be created using images of the pupils identifying when they are demonstrating stickability.

This session could be completed with a range of different scenarios using the further examples (on the **next two teaching slides**) or ones that you create yourself based on classroom experience. Ask the pupils:

Are they demonstrating stickability?

Pupils' responses

How are these connected?
- 'Because they all stick to everything except the sky.'
- 'Because they are all sticky.'
- 'Sticky tape has invisible glue.'

Does Arthur demonstrate stickability? Why do you think that?
- 'No, because he is refusing. He is not trying!'
- 'No, because he is giving up.'
- 'No. You can't give up on things if you find them difficult.'

What does Arthur need to do to show stickability?
- 'He needs to stop giving up and practise.'
- 'He needs to keep concentrating.'
- 'He needs to read his book to get better at reading.'
- 'Keep on trying.'
- 'Try sounding out the words.'
- 'I would keep encouraging him to practise.'
- 'Tell him not to give up!'

Does Jenna demonstrate stickability? Why do you think that?
- 'Yes, because she keeps on trying.'
- 'Yes, because she keeps on practising.'
- 'Yes, as she listened to her teacher and learnt how to do it.'

5 Being great

Summary

Using the book *The Littlest Yak* by Lu Fraser and Kate Hindley, this session encourages pupils to reflect on how a character is successful and to identify characteristics that contribute to their success.

Focus

Developing commitment and confidence

Outcome

To identify how someone (a character) is successful
To identify characteristics that make them successful

Resources

The Littlest Yak by Lu Fraser and Kate Hindley (2020)
Visualiser

Session

1. Arrange the pupils so they are sitting in a position where they can see the book clearly. Explain to the pupils that there are no right or wrong answers and that you are just interested in their opinions. Share an image of the front cover, using a visualiser if necessary, and ask the pupils to discuss:

   What do you notice about the character?

   Provide the pupils with some time to discuss and then take feedback from them.

2. You may need to provide some scaffolding for the discussions by asking some of the following questions:

   How is the small yak different from the others?
   Which yak would you like to be? Why?
   Which yak do you think is the toughest? Why do you think that?

   The pupils could share their opinions by a show of hands.

3. Explain to the pupils that you are going to read to them the book *The Littlest Yak* by Lu Fraser and Kate Hindley. Explain that you want them to concentrate carefully and listen to the story. While they are listening to the story you want them to think about:

   What is Gertie great at?

SESSIONS FOR 5–6-YEAR-OLDS (YEAR 1)

4. Read until page 12 and then ask the pupils to share their thoughts on:
   What is Gertie great at?
   If the pupils need support to identify what Gertie is great at you could zoom in on some of the illustrations, such as her reading a book, to illustrate the ideas (page 11).

5. Continue reading the story until the end. Ask the pupils to reflect on and then discuss:
   What did Gertie do in the story?
   What helped to make her successful at saving the tiniest yak?
   How did … help Gertie?

6. You could use the outline of a mountain with Gertie saving the tiniest yak written at the highest point to list what helped make Gertie successful in the story.

Follow up

This session could be used with a range of books, such as *Giraffes Can't Dance* by Giles Andreae (2014).

Pupils' responses

What do you notice about the character?
- 'The littlest one is in the middle of the others.'
- 'All the big yaks are together but the small one is on its own.'
- 'All the yaks are different.'
- 'The big yaks are wearing clothes but the small one isn't.'
- 'I think the little one is the main character.'
- 'The big ones have horns. The smallest one doesn't.'

Which yak would you like to be? Why?
- 'The big ones because they have the biggest horns.'
- 'The big yaks because they are big!'
- 'The small one because it will get tougher.'
- 'The small one because it can jump high.'
- 'My sister is small, and she is tough, so the small one.'

What is Gertie great at?
- 'Climbing up mountains.'
- 'Reading books.'
- 'Not staying still.'
- 'Eating vegetables.'
- 'Having grippy feet.'

What did Gertie do in the story?
- 'She realised that small yaks were great.'
- 'She helped a small yak who was stuck!'
- 'She saved someone.'

What helped to make her successful at saving the tiniest yak?
- 'Her feet because they were grippy.'
- 'Her smallness because she could fit in small places.'
- 'She was great at climbing.'
- 'She was brave.'

6 Words, words, words

Summary

This session encourages pupils to reflect on what we say to ourselves and others, our inner voice and how we can reframe our feedback.

Focus

Developing control and confidence

Outcome

To identify how certain words make us feel
To suggest other phrases that we should use to give feedback

Resources

Teaching slides: Year 1 Session 6
Handout: Say this

Session

1. Arrange the pupils so they are sitting with a talk partner and can see the board clearly.

2. Explain to the pupils that we are going to think about our inner voice – the voice inside of us that we can hear. Often this voice can be very negative; it talks about what we can't do and how rubbish we are. It is like a monster lurking inside all of us that appears when we are worried, facing new challenges or finding something tricky.

3. Explain to the pupils that you have been thinking about your own inner voice and the negative things it says to you. Using the **teaching slide**, share with the pupils an example of your inner voice.

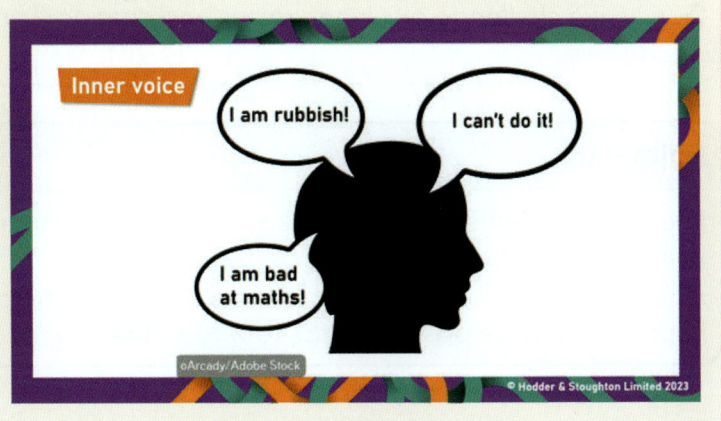

Sessions for 5–6-year-olds (Year 1)

4. Ask the pupils to discuss with their talk partner:
   How do the words make me/you feel?

5. Provide the pupils with some time to discuss their ideas with their partner and then take feedback. Probe the pupils' thinking further by asking them:
   Why does it make you feel like that?

6. Develop this further by asking the pupils to think about their own inner voice and reflect on what it says to them. Provide the pupils with some thinking time.

7. You may wish to ask some pupils to share their inner voice if they wish to. Be sensitive and ask for volunteers. It may be more appropriate to tell the pupils that they can share their inner voice with you if they wish to at another point.

8. Explain to the pupils that we need to challenge our inner voice when it is speaking in a negative way that makes us feel sad and prevents us from doing things.

9. Select an example of a negative inner voice and model how it can be challenged and reframed into a positive, e.g:
   'I am bad at maths' becomes 'I find maths tricky, but I am working hard and getting better at it.'
   Explain that, when we change our inner voice and use our positive voice, we can overcome difficulties and rise to new challenges.

10. Explain to the pupils that there are no right or wrong answers and that you are just interested in their opinions.

11. Together, look at the other examples of a negative inner voice and ask the pupils in turn to discuss with their talk partner what we should say instead when we are using our positive voice. You could use the **handout**. Ask:
    How can we challenge our inner voices and change 'I can't do it!' into a positive?
    Can we challenge our inner voices and change 'I am bad at maths' into a positive?

Follow up

Pupils can take their own examples of a negative inner voice and reframe them in a positive voice. They could use the **handout**.

A display could be created to reinforce how we should use our positive voice. Pupils could write positive cards to add to the display.

6 Words, words, words

Pupils' responses

How do the words make me/you feel?
Why does it make you feel like that?

> 'Disappointed.'

> 'Sad.'

> 'Angry – as you might think you are good at maths.'

> 'Worried – as if you had to try again you still might not be any good.'

Pupil's example

> 'When I wake up, my inner voice says I don't want to go to school because I can't do the work.'

How can we challenge our inner voices and change 'I can't do it!' into a positive?

> 'I am fabulous because I am trying.'

> 'I can do it!'

> 'Keep on doing it!'

> 'Keep on trying.'

> 'Don't listen to your inner voice.'

How can we challenge our inner voices and change 'I am bad at maths' into a positive?

> 'I can do maths; I won't give up.'

> 'I am good at maths.'

> 'Sometimes you need an extra box. Or help. Your glasses can be an extra box – they help you.'

you ont gud at it

Im not redey. IM not good

Say this...

Say this...

A pupil's response to
'Inner voice: I'm not good at it.'

A pupil's response to
'Inner voice: I'm not ready. I'm not good.'

67

SESSIONS FOR 5–6-YEAR-OLDS (YEAR 1)

7 Power of mistakes

Summary

This session encourages pupils to reflect on how to respond when we make a mistake and how to use the mistakes to help us grow and learn. It uses the context of maths and number bonds to 10.

Focus

Developing challenge and commitment

Outcome

To identify what we can learn from a mistake

To develop strategies to enable us to develop when we make a mistake

Resources

Teaching slides: Year 1 Session 7
Handout: What do you notice?
Handout: What can you learn?

Session

1. Arrange the pupils so they are sitting with their talk partner and can see the board.
2. Explain to the pupils that you have done some maths learning and would like them to review it.
3. Using the **first teaching slide** or the **What do you notice? handout**, share with the pupils the image of the calculation 3 + 7 = 9.

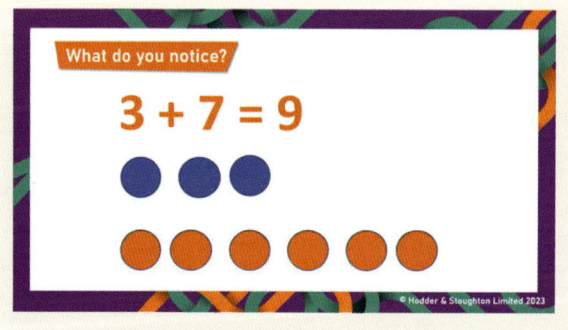

   What do you notice?

   $3 + 7 = 9$

4. Ask the pupils to discuss with their talk partner:
   What do you notice?

68

5. Take feedback from the pupils and probe their thinking further by listening to their responses and asking:

   Why do you think that?

   What do you think caused me to make that mistake?

6. Explain to the pupils that we all have brains and that these help us learn and that we are going to use this mistake to help grow our brains. Ask the pupils to think further about your mistake. Share the **next teaching slide** and pose the question:

   What can you learn from this?

7. Provide the pupils with some time to discuss what they can learn from the mistake and then gather their ideas. You could use the **What can you learn? handout**.

8. Develop the pupils' thinking further by asking them to imagine that they are your teacher and to think about how they would help you. Ask them to reflect on:

   If you were my teacher, what would you say?

   What would you do?

   How would you explain to me how to do 3 + 7?

   If I were feeling sad about a mistake, what would you say to me?

   During the discussions about how the teacher can support the pupils, they may suggest making the answer correct by changing the calculation. If they respond in this way, ensure that you challenge their thinking by asking:

   Will that help me to learn?

Follow up

This activity could be repeated in a range of contexts, e.g. when looking at different attempts at spelling a word.

During maths lessons this activity could be completed in different contexts to encourage pupils to learn from mistakes.

Pupils' responses

What do you notice?
- 'There is a 3 there, but you've only added 6.'
- 'That 3 + 7 doesn't equal 9.'
- '3 + 6 = 9 so you're wrong.'

What do you think caused me to make that mistake?
- 'You counted one of the dots twice.'
- 'You got distracted.'
- 'If you had 6 in the sum not a 7 the answer would be right.'

What can we learn from this?
- 'If you take 1 away, then it's 2 + 7 = 9'
- 'That 3 + 7 = 9 is not right. It's 10!'
- 'That you need to do your learning in a quiet room to concentrate.'
- 'That you need to count carefully.'
- 'That you should double check your answers.'

If you were my teacher, what would you say?
- 'Next time, I will help you as your number bonds to 10 are not right.'
- 'I would tell you to rub a counter out, so you were right!'
- '9 + 1 = 10, 8 + 2 = 10 so 3 + 7 = 10. I would help you learn the pattern.'

What would you do?
How would you explain to me how to do 3 + 7?
- 'I would teach you the number bonds song.'
- 'I would get you to count on from 7 on your fingers.'
- 'Use your knowledge to make a new number sentence.'

If I were feeling sad about a mistake, what would you say to me?
- 'It might be tricky but keep trying.'
- 'Don't be sad. You are learning when you make a mistake.'

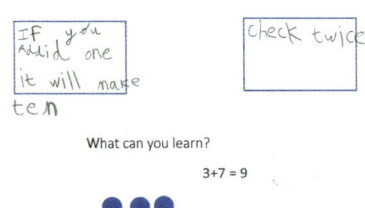

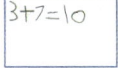

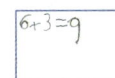

A pupil's response to 'What can you learn?'

8 My 4Cs

Summary

This session encourages pupils to reflect on the different aspects of mental toughness and create a profile of themselves.

Focus

Developing control, challenge, commitment and confidence

Outcome

To reflect and identify areas of strength
To identify next steps and how to respond to challenges

Resources

Handout: Profile template

Session

1. Arrange the pupils so they are sitting at a table and can clearly see you modelling on the board.
2. Explain to the pupils that they are going to reflect on the 4Cs and identify their strengths and areas to develop.
3. Begin by modelling something that you are confident at using the **handout**. Record this in the first box using words, pictures or a combination of both.
4. During this activity ensure that you share your thoughts and feelings explicitly with the pupils, e.g. *'I am great at maths – I have been working very hard and have got better. I can remember all of my number bonds.'* Make the connection to Session 5: Being great. Remind the pupils of the story of Gertie in *The Littlest Yak* and how they were able to identify her strengths.
5. Provide the pupils with some time to record the thing that they feel confident in and then randomly select a few pupils to share their thoughts.
6. Next explore the concept of commitment with the pupils. Link this to Session 4: Stickability. Model something that you are stuck on but keep working at, e.g. 'I am finding using the computer to make films tricky, but I am sticking at it as I want to improve'. Give the pupils some time to record the thing that they are showing commitment/stickability with and reinforce the concept by sharing some examples.

7 Then model reflecting on something that you find challenging, e.g. 'I would like to get better at drawing'. Explain to the pupils why you find it challenging and reinforce how this can make us feel. Record this on the board and then ask the pupils to record something that they find challenging.

8 Develop this further by asking the pupils to reflect on how you can respond and control your challenge. Model some different scenarios for the pupils:

I found art challenging, so I am going to practise my drawing.

I find learning to ride my bike challenging so I am going to keep my stabilisers on and practise.

I find answering take-aways challenging so I am going to ask my teacher to help me.

9 Distribute the **handouts**, provide the pupils with some time to complete their profile and then ask them to explain to a partner how they are going to control their challenges and improve. During these discussions, eavesdrop and then share some examples with the class. This will enable the pupils to see that everyone has challenges and needs to think about ways of overcoming them. Pupils often have the misconception that 'clever' children are just able to do things.

10 Explain to the pupils that we will revisit their profiles in the future and reflect on what has changed and why.

Follow up

Revisit the pupils' profiles and discuss with pupils how they have developed as individuals and as a class. You may wish to share the profiles at parents evening and ask the pupils to explain to their parents how they want to improve and develop, along with the areas in which they identify as being confident or showing commitment.

8 My 4Cs

Pupils' responses

Confidence — I am great at drawing. I stuck at bicribin (bike riding).
Challenge — I want to not crie. I will learn by wen I get...

confidence — climbing. I am great at...
challenge — get better at writing. stuck at reading, learn at school.

Confidnt — I am great at reading.
Challenge — I want to draw.
Commitment/stickability — I am stuck at comprenshon.
Control — keep tryig to drawing.

Pupils' responses to 'My 4Cs'

Sessions for 6–7-year-olds (Year 2)

Session	Focus	Outcomes	Summary	Page
1 Burst the bubble!	Developing control and confidence	To identify how we feel when we are worried To develop strategies to build resilience	This session explores how we feel and behave when we are worried. It encourages pupils to reflect on how they build firm foundations and strategies for overcoming challenges.	76
2 Step by step	Developing control and commitment	To reflect on how we feel when faced with a challenging task To sequence the steps to achieve a goal	This session reflects on how we feel when we are faced with a challenging task. It provides pupils with strategies to break down tasks into manageable small steps which enable them to achieve their goals.	79
3 My bank of strength	Developing control, challenge, commitment and confidence	To describe how we feel when things go wrong To reflect on how mistakes and challenges help us to build our mental strength	This session reflects on how responding and coping with setbacks helps to build our mental strength. It explores how dealing with our emotions and moving forward helps build our resilience and leads to success.	83

Session	Focus	Outcomes	Summary	Page
4 Stuck	Developing control and commitment	To identify strategies that we can use when stuck	This session explores how we feel when we are stuck and looks at practical strategies to help, using the context of learning spellings.	86
5 We are all different	Developing confidence	To identify how we are all unique	Using the book *A Little Bit Different* by Claire Alexander, this session explores our differences and how they are also our strengths.	89
6 I believe I can	Developing commitment and confidence	To identify an area in which to improve To reflect on the language we use to talk about ourselves	This session focuses on things that we can learn how to do and how we can commit to achieving them.	92
7 Pop, fizz, pop, fizz	Developing control	To identify strategies to help take control when we are feeling anxious and worried	This session explores how we can develop strategies to help pupils self-regulate when they are feeling anxious.	95
8 I excel at …	Developing control, challenge, commitment and confidence	To identify what makes you excel at something	This session asks pupils to identify something they excel at and explores what makes them excel at it.	98

Overview

The focus for the Year 2 sessions is developing practical strategies and approaches to worries, problems and challenges. Self-regulation is explored, individual differences are celebrated and confidence is developed through this and the chunking of challenges. Pupils' vocabulary is developed in a range of contexts and pupils are encouraged to share their own personal experiences.

SESSIONS FOR 6–7-YEAR-OLDS (YEAR 2)

1 Burst the bubble!

Summary

This session explores how we feel and behave when we are worried. It encourages pupils to reflect on how they build firm foundations and strategies for overcoming challenges.

Focus

Developing control and confidence

Outcome

To identify how we feel when we are worried
To develop strategies to build resilience

Resources

Teaching slides: Year 2 Session 1
Handout: Bubble template
Bubble mixture and bubble wand

Session

1. Using the **first teaching slide**, reveal the word 'worry' on the board and ask the pupils to discuss with their talk partner:
   What does the word 'worry' mean?
   Explain to the pupils that there are no right or wrong answers and that you are just interested in hearing their opinions. Listen carefully to the discussions and then ask pupils for feedback on their thoughts.

2. Develop the discussions further by posing the question:
   How do you behave when you are worried?
   You may ask the pupils to respond by answering the question or by demonstrating how they might behave:
   Tell me.
   Show me.
   Listen carefully to the discussions and then ask pupils for feedback on their thoughts.
   Using the **next teaching slide**, share with the pupils the image of a child blowing bubbles. Ask them:
   What is happening in the picture?
   Take feedback from the pupils.

3. Explain to the pupils that everyone has worries and concerns, and reassure them that is normal. Explain that we can use bubbles to represent these worries and concerns.

Visible Thinking

Model sharing something that you are worried about. Share how you feel and record your worry in a bubble.

4. Distribute the **handouts** and ask the pupils to record one of their worries in a bubble. If pupils do not have a worry at this time, you could ask them to record a worry from the past or something they think people worry about.

5. Once the pupils have recorded their worries in their bubbles, you could ask for volunteers to share their worries. It is important only to ask pupils who are happy to share their worries to do so.

6. Use the bubble mixture and bubble wand to blow some bubbles and ask someone else to pop the bubbles. Explain that they are helping you by popping your worries.

7. Ask the pupils to discuss with their talk partners:

   How we can manage our worries and 'burst the bubbles'?

   Can you think of practical ways in which we can help each other with our worries?

   Gather feedback from the pupils.

8. You may wish to develop the discussions further by focusing on one of the pupils' responses and asking the pupils to reflect more specifically on how they can support the pupil with their worry. Ask the pupils:

   What would you say to … if they were worried about …?

   What would you suggest they do?

Follow up

The pupils' worry bubbles could be displayed in the classroom along with the strategies for 'bursting the bubbles' and reducing their worries. This can be used as a reference point to reinforce the pupils' positive behaviours.

Pupils' responses

What does the word 'worry' mean?

> 'Being unsure about something.'
>
> 'You are scared of something that is going to happen. You don't want it to happen.'
>
> 'If you broke the rules, you'd be worried about being told off.'
>
> 'Worry means – you could be worried if you forgot to practise your maths and everyone else did.'
>
> 'Frightened.'

How do you behave when you are worried?

- 'You may be quiet.'
- 'Bite your nails.'
- 'Too scared to talk about it.'
- 'Not sleeping.'

How can we manage our worries and 'burst the bubbles'?

- 'Try to do something to overcome your worry – for example, try to make new friends.'
- 'Try thinking of happy things if you can't get to sleep.'
- 'Once you've tried something new it gets easier.'
- 'Talk to someone.'

What would you say to someone if they are worried about learning to tell the time?

- 'Practise.'
- 'Ask for help – from a teacher, friend or parent.'
- 'Try your best.'
- 'Tell someone.'

What would you say to someone if they are worried about your friend not being in school and having no one to play with?

- 'Tell them "other people can play with you and make you happy".'
- 'Make new friends – it's good to have lots of friends.'
- 'Don't worry – they might not be absent.'

What would you say to someone if they are worried about moving to a new house?

- 'Tell them "you'd get a new bedroom".'
- 'It could be exciting.'
- 'Talk to your parents/family.'

A pupil's bubble worry
'I struggle in maths a lot.'

A pupil's bubble worry
'We might move house!'

2 Step by step

Summary

This session reflects on how we feel when we are faced with a challenging task. It provides pupils with strategies to break down tasks into manageable small steps which enable them to achieve their goals.

Focus

Developing control and commitment

Outcome

To reflect on how we feel when faced with a challenging task

To sequence the steps to achieve a goal

Resources

Teaching slides: Year 2 Session 2

Handout: Steps to success template

Handout: Steps to success sorting activity

Session

1. In this activity you are going to model reacting to a challenging task. Arrange the pupils so they are sitting with a talk partner and can see you clearly. Model how you would react to having a challenging homework: share your frustration, stamp your feet, show reluctant body language, shout your frustration and tell the pupils 'I can't do it. It's too hard.'

2. Move out of role and ask the pupils:
   What did you see me do?
   What did you hear?
   How did I behave?
   What did I say?
   Provide the pupils with some time to reflect on these questions. You may wish to scaffold their thinking further by posing other questions.

3. Take feedback from the pupils and then develop their thinking further by asking:
   Why do you think I behaved in that way?
   Provide the pupils with some time for discussion and then take feedback.

4. Ask the pupils to reflect on:
   Have you ever behaved like this? If so, when and why?
   Again, take feedback.

SESSIONS FOR 6–7-YEAR-OLDS (YEAR 2)

Visible Thinking

Explain to the pupils that, when we are faced with challenging tasks, we often avoid doing them and can become frustrated. We behave like I did because we are worried about getting things wrong. We put our energy into our reactions not the task.

5. Using the **teaching slide** and the **Steps to success template handout**, share with the pupils the image of the steps and explain that we can take control of our challenges and that tasks can be broken down into smaller manageable steps that enable us to achieve and overcome challenges.

6. Using the scenario of having homework to do, share with the pupils some small steps that would lead to success. You may wish to adapt the activity to reflect the type of homework that you set, e.g. online learning.

7. After sharing the steps, you may wish to read each one to the pupils to ensure they understand them.

✂--
| Find somewhere quiet to concentrate. |
| If you find it tricky, ask for help. |
| Read the question carefully. |
| Check your answer. |
| Get your pencil and your book. |
| Answer the question. |

Steps to success sorting activity

8. Distribute the cut-out **Steps to success sorting activity handouts** and ask the pupils to work with a partner to sequence the steps on the template in an agreed order. Tell them to think carefully about the most effective order.

9. Remind them that they may have different ideas from their partner and that they need to discuss them carefully.

10. Provide the pupils with some time to order the steps and then ask:
    How did you order the steps?
    Select some pupils to explain how they have ordered the steps and why they chose to do it that way. There may be some slight variations in the order of the responses.

11. During the feedback, ensure that you reinforce asking for help once they have tried themselves.

2 STEP BY STEP

Follow up

Ask the pupils to reflect on whether they think there is a step missing from the activity.

Pupils can select a challenging activity and break it down into small achievable steps.

Step by step can be used as an approach to procedural success criteria in other learning contexts.

Pupils' responses

What did you see me do? What did you hear? How did I behave? What did I say?

'You gave up straight away.'
'You found it too hard, so you didn't want to do it.'
'You were so grumpy; you weren't going to do it!'
'You wanted to play on your games console.'
'You weren't bothered about your work.'
'If you behave like that you won't get on your games console.'
'You said it was 'too hard' but you didn't try.'
'You weren't being resilient.'
'You were stamping your feet.'
'You were moaning and groaning.'
'You didn't do any of your work.'
'You were being hard on yourself.'

How did you order the steps?

'Find somewhere quiet to concentrate.'
'Get your pencil and your book.'
'Read the question carefully.'
'Answer the question.'
'If you find it tricky, ask for help.'
'Check your answer.'

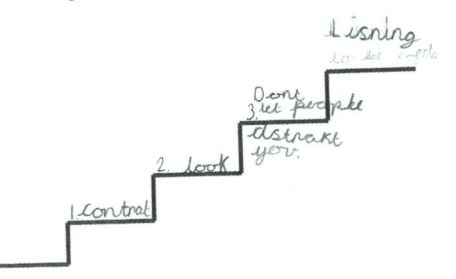

A pupil's steps to good listening

Sessions for 6–7-year-olds (Year 2)

> **Maths** (top step)
>
> have more paishents / go on tt rockstars more
>
> go on doke Maths more
>
> being brave when somtiny goes wrong

A pupil's steps to success in maths

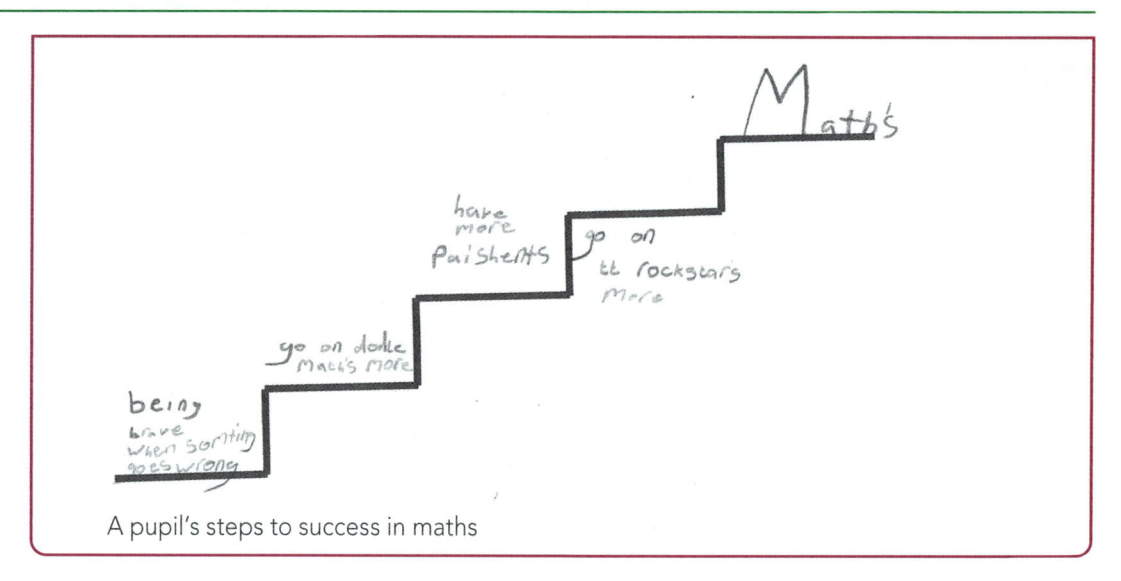

3 My bank of strength

Summary

This session reflects on how responding to and coping with setbacks helps to build our mental strength. It explores how dealing with our emotions and moving forward helps to build our resilience and leads to success.

Focus

Developing control, challenge, commitment and confidence

Outcome

To describe how we feel when things go wrong

To reflect on how mistakes and challenges help us to build our mental strength

Resources

Teaching slides: Year 2 Session 3
Handout: My bank of strength
An image of something going wrong (optional)

Session

1. Arrange the pupils so they are sitting with a partner and can see the board. Remind them that they need to listen carefully as you will be sharing your experiences.

2. Using either the **first teaching slide** or your own image, share with the pupils an image of a scenario in which something goes wrong. You could use photographs of yourself dealing with a particular problem or experience, e.g. baking a cake that goes wrong, failing to score a goal in football or falling out with friends. Modelling your own personal experiences helps to normalise the fact that everyone faces challenges and failures.

Visible Thinking

For example: I remember, when I was younger, doing a spelling test at school and everyone else scored really well, and I only got one correct. I was very upset because the rest of the class had done better than me. I went home and cried, and decided that I was going to give up. I struggled to remember my spellings even though I practised. When I was calmer, I spoke to my mum who offered to help me practise. I really wanted to get better and although I found it hard, I knew I could do better. Next time I did a test, my score was a little better.

SESSIONS FOR 6–7-YEAR-OLDS (YEAR 2)

3 Using the **next teaching slide**, share with the pupils the image of a piggy bank and ask them to talk to their talk partner:
What do we use this for? Why?

4 Explain to the pupils that we can build our resilience by responding positively to the challenges that we experience. Explain that we can collect these experiences in the same way that we save up our money in a money bank. Our bank of strength contains our mistakes and the challenges that we have overcome.

Visible Thinking

Model briefly some of the experiences that you have in your bank of strength, e.g:
- falling off your bike and getting back on it and riding it safely
- not doing well in your spelling test but learning your spellings and doing better in the next test
- losing in a game to your brother but choosing to play again.

5 Remind the pupils that we are all different and that we won't find the same things challenging.

Ask the pupils to reflect on:
What experiences would you put into your bank of strength?

Distribute the **handouts** and provide the pupils with some reflection time and then ask them to share them with their talk partner.

6 During the pupils' discussions eavesdrop on their conversations and collect examples to share with the class. This strategy will enable you to share the pupils' experiences.

Follow up

Pupils could record the key events that have contributed to their bank of strength on the **handout**. This could be completed retrospectively or as an ongoing log.

Create a class display of coins illustrating different experiences that have been added to the pupils' bank of mental strength.

Select a character from a known story and identify the experiences that have helped them develop their mental strength, e.g. the owl from *The Owl Who was Afraid of the Dark* by Jill Tomlinson (2014).

3 My bank of strength

Pupils' responses
What experiences would you put into your bank of strength?

'Making biscuits – we forgot to put an ingredient in, so they went wrong. So we started again.'

'I didn't know what to write but I kept thinking and stuck at it.'

'I am scared of heights, but I tried a ride at a theme park even though it was scary!'

My bank of strength

- Once I made a cake and I forgot to put eggs but I didn't give up
- Once I fell of my bike but I got back up
- Once I did a cartwheel and I fell over but I didn't give up
- When I was swimming I swoloed some water but I got back up
- Once I was doing my work but I made a mistake but I didn't give up
- When I was runing I fell over but I got back up

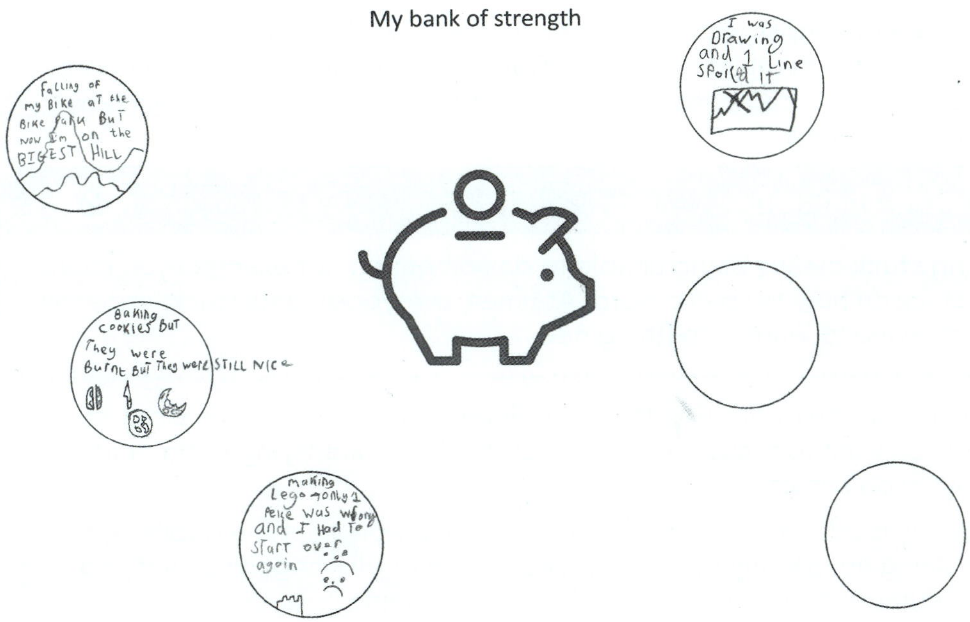

My bank of strength

- Falling of my bike at the bike park but now I'm on the BIGGEST HILL
- I was Drawing and 1 Line Spoilet it
- Baking cookies but they were burnt but they were still nice
- Making Lego 1 peice was wrong and I had to start over again

Pupils' responses to 'My bank of strength'

SESSIONS FOR 6–7-YEAR-OLDS (YEAR 2)

4 Stuck

Summary

This session explores how we feel when we are stuck and looks at practical strategies to help, using the context of learning spellings.

Focus

Developing control and commitment

Outcome

To identify strategies that we can use when stuck

Resources

Teaching slides: Year 2 Session 4
Handout: Stuck sorting activity

Session

1. Arrange the pupils so they can see the board and are sitting with a talk partner. It is easier if they sit at tables for the sorting activity.

2. Using the **first teaching slide**, reveal the word 'stuck' on the board and ask the pupils:

   What does the word 'stuck' mean?

   Provide the pupils with some thinking time and then ask them to discuss their ideas with their talk partner. During the discussions, eavesdrop on the conversations so that you can hear the pupils' perceptions and any misconceptions.

   ### Visible Thinking

   Being **stuck** means being unable to do something, for example you could be stuck on how to spell a word. At times, everybody gets stuck, especially when trying to learn something new.

3. Explain to the pupils that there are different meanings of the word 'stuck', but you want to focus on being stuck when you are trying to do or learn how to do something.

4. Silently model on the board trying to spell a word that the pupils find challenging. Silently modelling reduces the pupils' cognitive load and encourages them to focus on what you are doing.

4 STUCK

5. During the modelling you should attempt to spell the word several times and begin to get frustrated and cross out letters, roll your eyes, gesture and use appropriate facial expressions.

6. Explain to the pupils that you are stuck trying to spell a word and that you want to learn how to spell the word.

7. Ask the pupils to reflect on:

    Have you ever felt stuck?

    How did you feel?

    Select a few pupils to share their experiences, and then challenge their thinking further by asking:

    Is it a bad thing not to be able to do something?

    This question will reveal their perceptions of themselves and what they think of being wrong.

8. Share the **handout** with the pupils. Provide one handout between two. Read the ideas to the pupils and then read them together to ensure they can all understand them. You may wish to clarify the meaning of 'dictionary' before the pupils begin the task.

Ask for help.

Remember parts of the word you know.

Keep trying.

Ask a friend.

Shout!

Write an easier word.

Use a dictionary.

Handout: Stuck sorting activity

9. Explain to the pupils that we need to take control when we are stuck and use strategies to help us improve. Ask the pupils to cut up the handout and then sort the ideas into ones that will help them improve at spelling and those that won't.

10. Provide the pupils with some time to sort the ideas. Remind the pupils that they may have different opinions and ways of sorting them and that this is fine. You are just interested in their ideas.

11 Take feedback from the pupils about how they have sorted the statements. Select some of the statements to reflect on further:

Would shouting help?

Ask pupils to respond by showing thumbs up or thumbs down.

12 Ask the pupils to reflect on:

Should I try to spell an easier word or stop trying?

Provide some talk time and take feedback from the pupils. Explain the information in the Visible Thinking box to the pupils:

Visible Thinking

Use the **next teaching slide** to explain what neurons are. When we learn to do something and try to do things that are hard, our brains develop and grow. Our neurons fire and, as we learn new things, connections are made in our brains.

Follow up

Model using the different strategies to learn and practise the spellings.

Reinforce strategies that can be used when we are stuck in different contexts. This can be made into a class display.

Pupils' responses

Have you ever felt stuck? How did you feel?

'Sad and ashamed.'

'Annoyed.'

'Bad for yourself.'

'Angry.'

'Sad.'

'Cross.'

Is it a bad thing not to be able to do something?

'Sometimes, as people think you are not clever.'

'No, as you just have to try.'

'If it easy to do, then yes.'

'Not if it is hard.'

Would shouting help?

'No, you'll just look cross.'

'No, everyone will look at you.'

5 We are all different

Summary

Using the book *A Little Bit Different* by Claire Alexander, this session explores our differences and how they are also our strengths.

Focus

Developing confidence

Outcome

To identify how we are all unique

Resources

Teaching slides: Year 2 Session 5

A Little Bit Different by Claire Alexander (2021)

Session

1. Using the **teaching slide**, reveal the word 'different' on the board and ask the pupils to discuss with their talk partner:
   What does the word 'different' mean?
2. Take feedback from the pupils and together define what the word means.

> **Visible Thinking**
>
> **Different** means not the same, different from someone else. We can be different in lots of ways, for example the colour of our hair or the things we like doing.

3. Introduce the pupils to the book *A Little Bit Different* by Claire Alexander. This is a wonderful book that illustrates how we should celebrate our differences.
4. Read the book to page 6 where the characters have all made their 'ploof' and ask the pupils:
   What do you notice?
5. Take feedback from the pupils and then continue reading to page 10 where the character creates a 'shoof' and ask the pupils:
   What has happened?

SESSIONS FOR 6–7-YEAR-OLDS (YEAR 2)

6. Take feedback from the pupils and then continue to share the book to page 16. Then ask the pupils to discuss with their talk partner:
   How is the character feeling? Why?

7. Provide the pupils with some talk time and eavesdrop on their conversations. Then ask the pupils to share their thoughts.

8. Continue reading the book to the end and ask the pupils:
   What are the other characters thinking now?

9. Select a small number of pupils to share their ideas about how the characters' opinions have changed.

Visible Thinking

Explain to the pupils that:
We are all different and what makes us different can often be our strengths. I am different because …

10. Share with the pupils your own ploofer and shoof, which contain the things that make you different and special.

Follow up

Each pupil can create their own ploofer and shoof to illustrate how their differences make them special. A class display could be made to showcase everyone's differences.

You could hold a follow-up discussion on what helped the main character overcome being different.

The book is also great for a whole-school assembly. As a follow-up, all pupils can create their own ploofer and shoof.

Pupils' responses

What does the word 'different' mean?

'I think it means that you are not the same as another person.'

'We all have different voices.'

'You can be different; one person can wear glasses, and another won't.'

'Different can be like a camel – one has one hump another can have two.'

Ploof. What do you notice?

'It's the odd one out.'

'It's good to be different.'

'It can't do it.'

Shoof. What has happened?

'It made a rainbow one.'

'It's better.'

How is the character feeling? Why?

'Sad – because it's the odd one out.'

'Sad – because the others were rude and made fun.'

'The others don't like it.'

'The others might be jealous as they can't do it.'

'Feels invisible.'

'Feels different.'

What are the other characters thinking now?

'They think it's beautiful, especially the heart.'

'They are amazed.'

'Sad as they were rude.'

'Surprised.'

Pupils' ploofers

SESSIONS FOR 6–7-YEAR-OLDS (YEAR 2)

6 I believe I can

Summary

This session focuses on things that we can learn how to do and how we can commit to achieving them.

Focus

Developing commitment and confidence

Outcome

To identify an area in which to improve

To reflect on the language we use to talk about ourselves

Resources

Teaching slides: Year 2 Session 6

I Believe I Can by Grace Byers (2020) (optional)

Session

1. Arrange the pupils so they can see the board and are sitting with their talk partner.

2. Share with the pupils the **first teaching slide** that states, 'I believe I can'. Read the statement to the pupils twice and then ask them to reflect on:

   What does 'I believe I can' mean?

   Provide the pupils with some thinking time and then ask them to share their thoughts with their talk partner.

3. Take feedback from the pupils and then clarify the meaning of the statement.

> **Visible Thinking**
>
> **'I believe I can'** means that if, for example, you were going to play a tennis match, you would believe that you could win. We all believe that we can do different things, e.g. I believe that I can draw.

4. Share with the pupils the image 'I can't' on the **next teaching slide** and ask the pupils:

   What do you notice in the image?

   Take feedback from the pupils and then develop their thinking further by asking:

   Why has this happened?

   What does it mean?

6 | BELIEVE I CAN

5. Take feedback from the pupils and then encourage them to reflect on their personal experiences:
   Have you ever felt like you couldn't do something?
   Have you ever said, 'I can't do it!'?
   Select a few pupils to share their own experiences and how they felt when they couldn't do something.

6. Using the **next teaching slide**, share the 'We can' image of three famous people who have been told that they can't do something and have succeeded. You may wish to personalise the slide to include people whom the pupils can relate to, are interested in or are topical.

   We can!

   © Hodder & Stoughton Limited 2023

7. Using the **next three teaching slides**, explain to the pupils briefly the experiences of the famous people:
   Walt Disney – was rejected 300 times by financiers for Mickey Mouse and his theme park. He was also told that by the newspaper he worked for that 'he lacked creativity' and he was then fired.
   James Dyson – the inventor and creator of the Dyson vacuum. He had 5126 failed attempts before he was successful at creating it.
   Emma Raducanu – had to drop out of Wimbledon 2021 due to a medical problem but went on to win the US Open later that year.

   ### Visible Thinking
   All of these famous people were told that they would not be successful at something they wanted to achieve. Yet, they overcame the challenges. Share your own experiences about something that you wanted to be able to do but were told you would not be successful at.

8. Develop this further by asking the pupils to think about something that they want to learn how to do and how to overcome barriers. These could be recorded and displayed in the classroom.

SESSIONS FOR 6–7-YEAR-OLDS (YEAR 2)

> **Follow up**
>
> *I Believe I Can* by Grace Byers reinforces the concept and uses wonderful imagery and language. This could be used as a shared text to explore the ideas from the session.

Pupils' responses

What does 'I believe I can' mean?

> 'It means you can do it.'
>
> 'You believe you can play football.'

What do you notice in the image? Why has this happened?

> 'You've changed the words.'
>
> 'It means you can do it.'
>
> 'Because we are talking about what we can do.'

Have you ever felt like you couldn't do something?

> 'When I was about to play a football match.'
>
> 'In basketball last week, I thought the girls' team couldn't win but they did!'
>
> 'When I was struggling to write a hard word.'

I can learn to ...riteatrickyworde

A pupil's response to 'I can learn to … write tricky words.'

I can learn to tell the time.

A pupil's response to 'I can learn to … tell the time.'

7 Pop, fizz, pop, fizz

Summary

This session explores how we can develop strategies to help pupils self-regulate when they are feeling anxious.

Focus

Developing control

Outcome

To identify strategies to help take control when we are feeling anxious and worried

Resources

Bottle of a fizzy drink

Session

1. Arrange the pupils so they are sitting in a circle.
2. Ask the pupils to think about:
   Have you ever been worried about not being able to do something?
   Provide the pupils with some thinking time and then ask them to share their experiences.
3. Use a bottle of a fizzy drink to represent you and your worries. Model becoming fizzy because you are worried about doing something. Every time you describe a problem or a behaviour, shake the bottle.

Visible Thinking

I am worried about learning to ride my bike. I am worried that I will fall off, that I won't be able to do it, that I might hurt myself, that my feet will get stuck, that my dad will be cross if I crash my bike, that I could hit a car, that my stomach hurts. All I can think about are my worries. I feel sick and I don't think I can do it!

4. Pass the bottle around the circle and ask the pupils to shake it and add to your worries.

Sessions for 6–7-year-olds (Year 2)

5. Ask the pupils to reflect on:
   What has happened to the bottle and me?
   Provide the pupils with some time to discuss their thinking with their peers and then take feedback from them.

6. Develop the pupils' thinking further by asking them:
   What will happen if I open the bottle?
   Take feedback from the pupils.

7. Explain to the pupils:

> ### Visible Thinking
> When I am worried about something and I keep my worries inside of me I feel like I am about to explode, and everything is going to come out. Every time I worry, my worries seem to grow.

8. Explain to the pupils that we need to take control of our worries and that there are things we can do to take control of how we are feeling. Ask the pupils to reflect on:
   How can we take control of how we are feeling?
   What can we do to make us feel better when we are worried?

9. Provide the pupils with some thinking time and then ask them to discuss their ideas with their partner. You may wish to model potential strategies to stimulate the discussion, e.g. talking to someone about your worries.

10. Take feedback from the pupils and create a list of useful strategies that can be displayed in the classroom. Reiterate the pupils' ideas as you model letting a small amount of air out of the bottle until it is no longer fizzy. Ask:
    What have we done?

Follow up
Create a display of ways of overcoming worries.

Pupils' responses

Have you ever been worried about not being able to do something?
> 'I was worried that if I played football, we would lose.'
> 'I was worried at first that I wouldn't be able to jump in the swimming pool.'

What has happened to the bottle and me?
> 'You have anger inside.'
> 'Your worries are fizzing inside.'

Pupils' responses

Have you ever been worried about not being able to do something?

'I was worried that if I played football, we would lose.'

'I was worried at first that I wouldn't be able to jump in the swimming pool.'

What has happened to the bottle and me?

'You have anger inside.'

'Your worries are fizzing inside.'

What will happen if I open the bottle?

'It will explode.'

'It will spray everywhere.'

'Your worries will come out.'

'You'll get wet!'

How can we take control of how we are feeling?
What can we do to make us feel better when we are worried?

'Breathing slowly in and out.'

'Talk about it!'

'Stop thinking about your worries.'

'Have a hug.'

'Do something you enjoy.'

'Have some quiet time.'

'Listen to music.'

What have we done?

'Let a little bit out at a time.'

SESSIONS FOR 6–7-YEAR-OLDS (YEAR 2)

8 I excel at …

Summary

This session asks pupils to identify something they excel at and explores what makes them excel at it.

Focus

Developing control, challenge, commitment and confidence

Outcome

To identify what makes you excel at something

Resources

Teaching slides: Year 2 Session 8
Images of things that the pupils might excel at (optional)

Session

1. Arrange the pupils so they are sitting in a circle. Any images should be placed in the centre of the circle so that all of the pupils can see them. Alternatively, if using the examples on the **first teaching slide**, make sure everyone can see this clearly.

2. Ask the pupils to think about something they excel at. Provide some thinking time and then go around the circle asking each pupil to share something they believe that they excel at. You may wish to model sharing what you excel at in a clear sentence and encourage the pupils to speak in clear sentences.

3. Develop the pupils' thinking further by asking them to think about:
What makes you excel at … [chosen area]?
Remind the pupils that there are no right or wrong answers and that you are just interested in their opinions.

4. Provide the pupils with some thinking time and then ask them to share their thoughts.

5. Split the pupils into small groups and explain that they are going to think about what makes you excel at a specific thing. As a group, they should gather all their ideas.

6. Before the pupils begin their discussions, you may wish to scaffold this activity as follows:

Visible Thinking

I think being good at challenging yourself means that you are willing to try new things, that you have a go and don't worry about making mistakes, that you will have go at things that are tricky and that you will ask for help if you are stuck.

7. Allocate the focuses for the pupils' discussions and provide them with some time to reflect on what makes them excel at … (e.g. listening, concentrating, sharing).
8. The pupils may wish to record their thoughts on paper. During the discussions, the pupils should be identifying behaviours and indicators that make them successful at something.
9. You should eavesdrop on the discussions and pick up on any misconceptions and address these during the feedback from the groups.

Follow up

The discussions could focus on the 4Cs and what makes you successful at these. An image of the 4Cs can be found on the **next teaching slide**.

Create visual reminders (success criteria) for behaviours that make you excel at … These could be reinforced with images of the pupils behaving in this way.

Pupils' responses

What makes you excel at listening?
- 'Sitting down.'
- 'Sharing and taking turns.'
- 'I like to listen when someone reads to me.'
- 'Looking at the person.'
- 'Asking questions.'

What makes you excel at concentrating?
- 'Doing something I like.'
- 'Looking at it.'
- 'Drawing – as I like it.'

What makes you excel at sharing?
- 'If someone helps me.'
- 'Taking it in turns.'
- 'Playing with friends.'
- 'Remembering it is a kind thing to do.'

Sessions for 7–8-year-olds (Year 3)

Title	Focus	Outcomes	Summary	Page
1 I have learnt to …	Developing control, challenge, commitment and confidence	To identify skills/knowledge that we have effectively learnt To identify what helps us to learn effectively	This session encourages pupils to think about young children and how they become learners and acquire knowledge and skills. This session reinforces the idea that we are always learning and that learning is incremental and mistakes are part of the process.	102
2 Worry spectrum	Developing control, challenge, commitment and confidence	To explore worries practically To identify which worries are significant to each individual	Using the concept of a spectrum, this session asks pupils to reflect on some potential worries and to identify those that they find most challenging.	105
3 Looking at things differently	Developing control, challenge, commitment and confidence	To reflect on how we view and respond to situations and problems	Using real-life scenarios, this session encourages pupils to look at things differently.	108

Overview

Title	Focus	Outcomes	Summary	Page
4 Yet	Developing control, challenge, commitment and confidence	To explore how language can impact on our perceptions	This session explores the power of the concept of 'yet' and how we should see our own development as a journey.	111
5 A really hard thing	Developing control, challenge, commitment and confidence	To reflect on how our problems can be viewed over time	This session uses images to represent our problems and the factors that help us deal with our feelings.	115
6 You choose	Developing control	To reflect on how we can control our responses to challenges	Using the context of a quiz, this session asks pupils to reflect on how they could take control and respond to challenges.	120
7 Erupting	Developing control	To explore how we can control our reactions	Using the image of a volcano, this session reflects on how our behaviours and emotions can overwhelm us.	126
8 Perfect recipe	Developing control, challenge, commitment and confidence	To plan how we would approach a challenge	Using the concept of a recipe, this session asks pupils to reflect on a personal challenge and to plan their approach.	130

Overview

The focus for the Year 3 sessions is exploring all of the 4Cs in different contexts. The sessions encourage pupils to look at things differently, while providing practical strategies to support them. A key aspect of the sessions is challenges and how we control and focus our reactions. The pupils are encouraged to develop self-regulation through the 4Cs.

SESSIONS FOR 7–8-YEAR-OLDS (YEAR 3)

1 I have learnt to …

Summary

This session encourages pupils to think about young children and how they become learners and acquire knowledge and skills. This session reinforces the idea that we are always learning and that learning is incremental and mistakes are part of the process.

Focus

Developing control, challenge, commitment and confidence

Outcome

To identify skills/knowledge that we have effectively learnt
To identify what helps us to learn effectively

Resources

Teaching slides: Year 3 Session 1
Handout: Reflections
Visualiser

Session

1. Arrange the pupils so they are sitting with a partner and can see the board clearly.
2. Using the **teaching slide**, share with the pupils an image of a baby and ask them to think about:
   What can a baby do when it is born?
3. Provide the pupils with some thinking time and then select some pupils to share their thoughts.
4. Deepen the pupils' thinking further by asking them to think about:
   What does a baby learn to do?
5. Provide the pupils with some thinking time and then ask them to discuss with a talk partner and identify five different things that a baby will have to learn to do.
6. Eavesdrop on the pupils' discussions and create a list on the board of the different things a baby has to learn to do.

102

7 Share the list with the pupils and then develop the pupils' thinking further by asking them to reflect on:
   What helps a baby to learn new skills?
8 Provide the pupils with some thinking time and then ask them to discuss their ideas with a talk partner.
9 Take feedback from the pupils and then ask them to reflect on what they have learnt to do. Ask:
   What helped you to learn?
10 Provide them with the **handout** and ask them to record four different things that they are proud that they have learnt to do. This activity will encourage the pupils to reflect on their own learning journey and reinforce the idea that learning is incremental and that mistakes are part of the process.
11 Select a small number of pupils to share what they have learnt and place the pupils' images under a visualiser so that everyone can see them clearly.
12 Ask each pupil to share what they have learnt and what helped them to learn effectively.

Follow up

Ask the pupils to reflect on what was the hardest thing they have had to learn and why.

Use the books *The Book of Mistakes* by Corinna Luyken (2017) and *The Wonderful Things You Will Be* by Emily Winfield Martin (2015) to explore the key concepts of learning, mistakes and future possibilities.

Pupils' responses

What can a baby do when it is born?

'Not very much.'

'They can cry!'

What does a baby learn to do? What helps a baby to learn new skills?

'Copying.'

'Someone teaching them.'

What helped you to learn?

'Someone who could do it already. They showed me. (Cousin, dad, friend)'

'My teacher, Mrs Fraser, helped me to learn how to write.'

'Watching someone who could do it already.'

Sessions for 7–8-year-olds (Year 3)

achery

Bakeing

I have learnt to...

Swimming

Danceing

Playing the piano

solving a Rubix cube

I have learnt to...

to swim

to write

Pupils' responses to 'I have learnt to …'

104

2 Worry spectrum

Summary

Using the concept of a spectrum, this session asks pupils to reflect on some potential worries and to identify those that they find most challenging.

Focus

Developing control, challenge, commitment and confidence

Outcome

To explore worries practically

To identify which worries are significant to each individual

Resources

Teaching slides: Year 3 Session 2
Handout: Worry spectrum
Handout: Worry scenarios

Session

1. Arrange the pupils so they are sitting with a partner and each have their own copy of both **handouts**. Ensure the spectrum is arranged with the red section at the top and the purple section at the bottom.

2. Using the **first teaching slide**, share with the pupils the word 'worry' and ask them to discuss with a partner what it means. *What does the word 'worry' mean?*

3. Provide the pupils with some talk time and then take feedback from them.

4. Using the **next teaching slide**, share with the pupils the image of the spectrum and explain that this spectrum can be use d to explore our worries. Explain that the red represents our biggest worries and that, as the colours fade, they represent our smaller worries. Explain that worries are very personal and what can be a large worry for one person may not be for another. Explain that we are all individuals and therefore have different worries.

5. Share with the pupils the list of worries on the **handout**. Read them to the pupils while they track the text with their finger. They should then read the worries with you and finally read them to you.

Worry spectrum

> - You are finding your maths homework too hard.
> - Your pet has been lost.
> - You are going on an overnight school trip.
> - You have to perform in front of others and are scared that they will laugh at you.
> - You have fallen out with your friend.
> - You have accidentally broken your friend's toys and are worried about telling them.
> - You are worrying about being late to school.

Worry scenarios

6. Explain to the pupils that you would like them to think about the different worries and then cut up the worry scenarios handout and place the scenarios on the worry spectrum. Remind the pupils that we are all different and that we all have different things that are bigger worries to us as individuals.

7. Remind the pupils that they should place their biggest worries on the red part of the spectrum and the smaller worries on the purple section.

8. Explain to the pupils that, if one of the scenarios does not worry them, they don't need to include it on their spectrum, e.g. if they don't have a pet, they won't be worried about losing it.

9. Provide the pupils with some time to sort their worries.

10. When some of the pupils are beginning to complete the task, pause the class and explain that they can personalise their worry spectrum and add their own worries whatever they may be.

11. Give the pupils a few more minutes and circulate around the classroom noting which worries have been identified as significant, then bring the class back together.

12. Share with the pupils your sorting of the worries. Focus on a worry that most of the pupils have identified as significant and ask them to think about:
Why is this worry important?

13. Take feedback from the pupils and then develop their thinking further by asking them:
How can you make your biggest worry smaller?

14. Provide the pupils with some talk time and again take feedback from them. The focus of reducing our worries will be explored further in Session 5: A really hard thing.

15. Once you have completed the activity you may wish to meet with some individual pupils to provide them with the opportunity to discuss their worries further.

Follow up

Have a worry box in the classroom and regularly revisit the worries in it through whole-class and individual discussions. During these discussions ensure that you acknowledge that the worries identified are legitimate and then explore how they should be approached.

Pupils' responses

What does the word 'worry' mean?

- *'You are concerned about something.'*
- *'If it is the first time you are doing something so you might be worried about it.'*
- *'Stressed about something.'*
- *'Nervous.'*
- *'Scared.'*
- *'You are scared that you won't be able to do something.'*
- *'Being worried can make you sad.'*

Why is this worry important?

- *'You have to perform in front of others and are scared that they will laugh at you.'*
- *'As it is important.'*
- *'It is special.'*
- *'No one wants to be embarrassed.'*

Think about your biggest worry. How can you make it smaller?

- *'Just do it!'*
- *'Learn from it if it goes wrong.'*
- *'Talk to someone.'*
- *'Know it is okay for things to go wrong. It happens to everyone.'*

SESSIONS FOR 7–8-YEAR-OLDS (YEAR 3)

3 Looking at things differently

Summary

Using real-life scenarios, this session encourages pupils to look at things differently.

Focus

Developing control, challenge, commitment and confidence

Outcome

To reflect on how we view and respond to situations and problems

Resources

Teaching slides: Year 3 Session 3

Session

1. Arrange the pupils so they are sitting with a partner and can see the board clearly.
2. Share with the pupils the image on the **first teaching slide** and ask them to think about:

   What do you see?

3. Take feedback from the pupils and then reiterate their thoughts aloud and emphasise that it is a negative experience and that the child should probably not try again.
4. Using the **next teaching slide,** share the image and explain to the pupils that we are going to put our glasses on in order to look at things differently. You may wish to provide the pupils with a template of the glasses so they can wear them and reinforce the idea that we are looking at things differently.
5. Return to the image of the child who has fallen off their bike and model looking at things differently.

3 Looking at things differently

> **Visible Thinking** 👁
>
> I see a boy who is trying very hard. He is learning to ride his bike and being brave and not letting his worries stop him. The girl is being kind and taking care of the boy.

6. Ask the pupils to think carefully about what you have said and how this viewpoint differs from the original one. Repeat the different viewpoint and then ask the pupils to discuss:
   How do the viewpoints differ?

7. Provide the pupils with some thinking time and then ask them to share their thoughts.

8. Display the **next teaching slide**, which shows a calculation containing a mistake:

> **What do you see?**
>
> **Rounding to the nearest 10**
>
> **372 ⟶ 380**
>
> © Hodder & Stoughton Limited 2023

9. Ask the pupils to think about their normal reaction and ask them:
   What do you see?

10. Take feedback from the pupils and then share the slide with the glasses on again or ask the pupils to put on their glasses and look at the image again. Again, ask the pupils:
    What do you see now you are wearing your glasses?

11. Provide the pupils with some thinking time and then ask them to discuss their ideas with their partner.

12. Take feedback from the pupils and reinforce the positives that they have identified.

13. Explain to the pupils that they can use the 4Cs to help them look at things differently.

14. Using the **next teaching slide**, share the poster of the 4Cs and recap on their meaning.

SESSIONS FOR 7–8-YEAR-OLDS (YEAR 3)

15 Ask the pupils to reflect on:
How can the 4Cs help you look at things differently?

16 Provide the pupils with some thinking time and then ask them to discuss their ideas with their talk partner.

17 Take feedback from the pupils.

Follow up

Adapt the lesson to include scenarios that are appropriate for your class and focus on issues/problems that they need to look at differently.

Use the idea of looking differently in other subjects to reinforce the concept.

Pupils' responses

What do you see?

Bicycle accident
> 'A sad boy, who has hurt himself.'
> 'He has tried to ride his bike but failed.'
> 'He can't ride his bike.'

How do the viewpoints differ?
> 'The second one is more positive.'
> 'The second one looks at the good.'
> 'The second one is about learning.'

What do you see?

Rounding error
> 'The answer is wrong.'
> 'They have made a mistake.'

What do you see now you are wearing your glasses?
> 'Someone is learning how to round.'
> 'They have tried to answer the question.'

How can the 4Cs help you look at things differently?
> 'You can think about how you can be committed and try again.'
> 'You can use your confidence to see that you keep trying.'
> 'You look at it positively and take control.'
> 'You can see them as challenges, things that you can try and learn to do.'

4 Yet

Summary

This session explores the power of the concept of 'yet' and how we should see our own development as a journey.

Focus

Developing control, challenge, commitment and confidence

Outcome

To explore how language can impact on our perceptions

Resources

Teaching slides: Year 3 Session 4
The Magical Yet by Angela DiTerlizzi (2020)
Visualiser

Session

1. Arrange the pupils so they can see the board clearly and are sitting with a partner.
2. Reveal the word 'yet' on the **first teaching slide** and ask the pupils to reflect on what it means.
   What does the word 'yet' mean?
   Remind the pupils that there are no right or wrong answers and that you are just interested in their opinions.

> **Visible Thinking**
>
> **Yet** means that something has not happened, for example 'I haven't learnt how to tie my shoelaces yet'.

3. Take feedback from the pupils and encourage them to listen to what each person says and to 'bounce off' their thoughts. Bouncing is a useful strategy as it encourages pupils to listen actively and then build or respond to the other person's ideas. Pupils can be taught phrases to use to support this strategy (see 'Key language' on pages 2–3).

4 Share with the pupils the **next teaching slide** containing the two sentences:
I can't do it!
I can't do it yet!

5 Ask the pupils to think about:
What is different?
Provide the pupils with some thinking time and then take feedback.

6 Develop the pupils' thinking further by asking them to reflect on:
How does the word 'yet' make you feel?

7 Provide the pupils with some thinking time and then ask them to share their thoughts with a peer. Then select pupils to share their ideas with the class.

8 Introduce the book *The Magical Yet* by Angela DiTerlizzi. The story uses the ideas that you have to learn how to do things, to try again and to commit to what you want to achieve.

9 You may wish to share the book using a visualiser as this will enable the pupils to see clearly and be able to focus on illustrations.

10 Read the book to page 12 after the Magical Yet has been introduced.

11 Explain to the pupils that 'yet' is a very powerful piece of language that can have a huge impact on how we see, cope with and respond to things.

12 Ask the pupils to imagine that 'yet' is a creature and to think about:
What does 'yet' look like?
What would 'yet' say?
What would 'yet' do?

13 Provide the pupils with some time to think about these questions. You may wish to display them on the board to act as a prompt for the pupils.

14 Provide the pupils with some time to create their version of 'yet', reminding them to include things that 'yet' would say.

15 Share examples of the pupils' 'yets' and ask them to explain carefully why they have created them in this way.

Follow up

Continue reading the book and ask the pupils to collect the things that yet has helped with.

Continue reading the book and ask the pupils to listen out for and collect the behaviours that contribute to the success of yet. These could be linked to the 4Cs.

4 Yet

Pupils' responses

What does the word 'yet' mean?

'Not now – maybe later.'

'You can't do something at the moment, but you will be able to do it in the future.'

What is different?

'One is negative about yourself.'

'One is positive.'

'One is about not being able to do something, the other is about being able to.'

'First one, that you don't believe that you can do it. But the second believes you can in the future when you have practised.'

How does the word 'yet' make you feel?

'Confident – like you can do it!'

'Makes you believe in yourself.'

'Optimistic – like I can learn my new piano piece.'

'That I could be successful.'

'Improves my self-esteem and makes me more confident.'

Magical, Kind

KEEP TRYING

Yet

Keep on trying!

The Sun Of Happiness

Don't give up!!!

No matter how hard it is don't give up!

113

Sessions for 7–8-year-olds (Year 3)

Pupils' 'yets'

5 A really hard thing

Summary

This session uses images to represent our problems and the factors that help us deal with our feelings.

Focus

Developing control, challenge, commitment and confidence

Outcome

To reflect on how our problems can be viewed over time

Resources

Teaching slides: Year 3 Session 5
Handout: A really hard thing

Session

1. Arrange the pupils so they can see the board and are sitting with their talk partner.
2. Share the image on the **teaching slide** and ask the pupils to look at it closely and reflect on:
   What do you notice?
   How does this image reflect how we feel about our problems?

A really hard thing

© Hodder & Stoughton Limited 2023

115

3. Provide the pupils with the **handout** and some time to think and then discuss their ideas with their partner. During their discussions, eavesdrop on the conversations and collect their ideas.

4. Ask the pupils to feed back their ideas to the class. You may wish to annotate the image with their ideas.

5. Share with the pupils that this image reflects how we feel about our problems/hard things over time. Explain that initially a problem can feel insurmountable and overwhelming but that gradually over time this reduces, and it becomes a small challenge until eventually it is no longer important to us.

Visible Thinking

At first, I was very worried about going to a new swimming class. I felt very anxious, my stomach kept turning over and I felt sick. I wasn't sleeping. After I had been to my first lesson, I was a little less worried. I felt more confident.

6. Taking each stage in turn, ask the pupils to discuss with their talk partner:
   How would you feel at stage 1?
   Which words would describe your emotions?

7. Provide the pupils with some time to discuss their ideas and then take feedback from them.

8. You may wish to annotate the image with the vocabulary to describe the emotions, writing it into the first circle.

9. Repeat for the next stage. Ask the pupils to discuss with their talk partner:
   How would you feel at stage 2?
   Which words would describe your emotions?

10. Provide the pupils with some time to discuss their ideas and then take feedback from them.

11. You may wish to annotate the image with the vocabulary to describe the emotions, writing it into the second circle.

12. Finally, ask the pupils to reflect on the final stage:
    How would you feel at stage 3?
    Which words would describe your emotions?

13. Develop the pupils' thinking further by asking them to reflect on:
    What helps us to reduce our feelings and worries about a hard thing/problem?
    Explain to the pupils that there are no right or wrong answers and that you are just interested in their thoughts. Explain that we are all different and therefore different things will help us.

14 Again, provide thinking time for the pupils and then ask them to discuss their ideas with their partner.

15 Select pupils to provide you with their thoughts and annotate the image in a different coloured pen to capture their ideas. You may wish to probe their thinking further by asking them:
How would this help you?

Follow up

Ask the pupils to reflect on their own situations and something really hard that they had to deal with. They should then record their feelings, emotions and strategies.

Create a class display to reinforce the emotions and strategies that can be used.

Pupils' responses

How does this image reflect how we feel about our problems?

- *'They start off big but then they get better.'*
- *'The problem or the hard thing is getting better or smaller.'*
- *'There's one without a circle and I think that's got better and it's easier to do it now.'*

SESSIONS FOR 7–8-YEAR-OLDS (YEAR 3)

How would you feel at each stage? Which words would describe your emotions? What helps us to reduce our feelings and worries about a hard thing/problem?

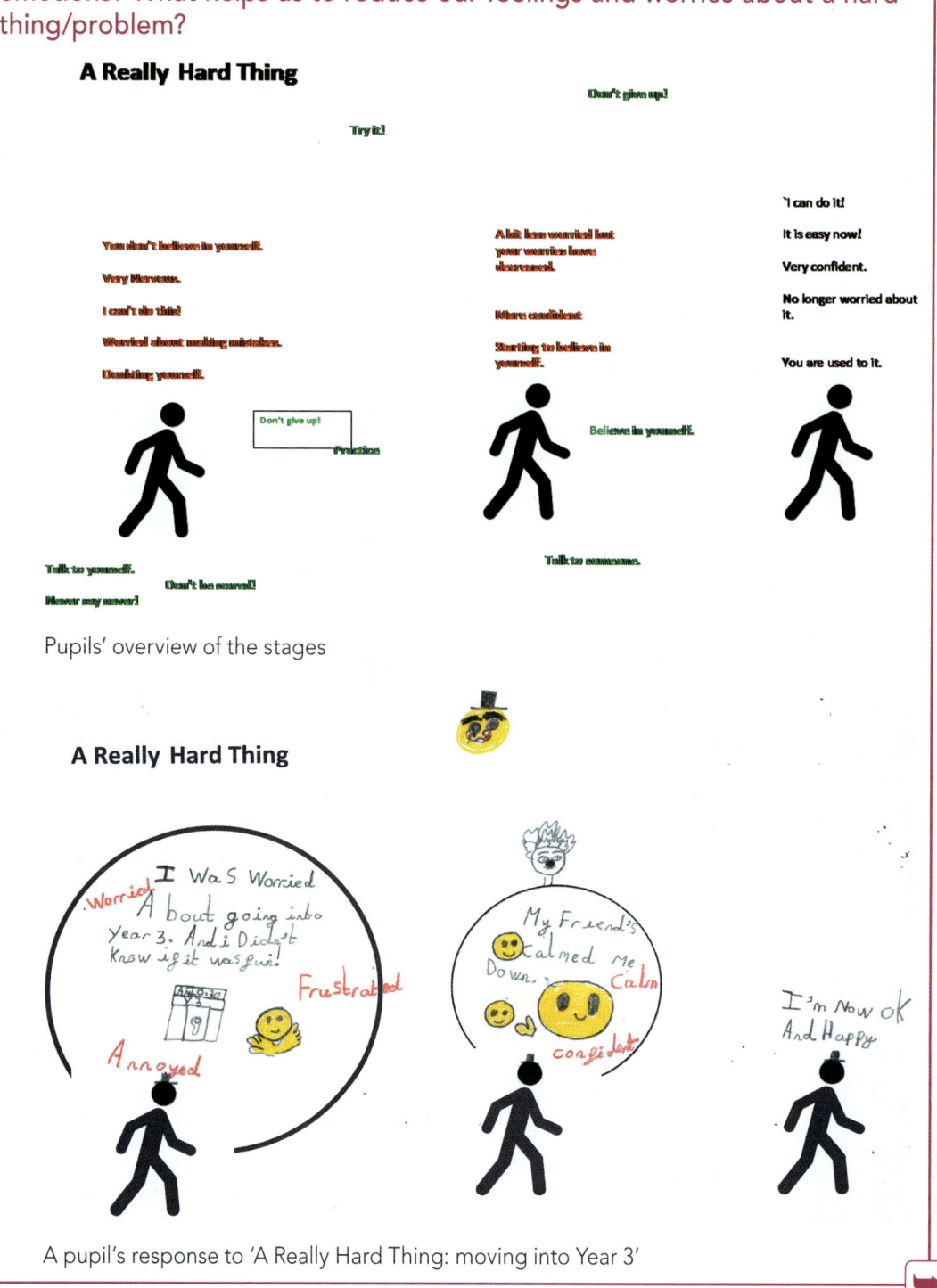

A Really Hard Thing

Try it!

Don't give up!

You don't believe in yourself.
Very Nervous.
I can't do this!
Worried about making mistakes.
Doubting yourself.

A bit less worried but your worries have decreased.

More confident.
Starting to believe in yourself.

'I can do it!
It is easy now!
Very confident.
No longer worried about it.
You are used to it.

Don't give up!
Practice.

Believe in yourself.

Talk to yourself..
Never say never!
Don't be scared!

Talk to someone.

Pupils' overview of the stages

A Really Hard Thing

Worried — I was worried about going into Year 3. And i didn't know if it was fun!
Annoyed
Frustrated

My Friend's calmed Me Down.
Calm
confident

I'm Now oK And Happy

A pupil's response to 'A Really Hard Thing: moving into Year 3'

5 A REALLY HARD THING

A Really Hard Thing

A pupil's response to 'A Really Hard Thing: moving to a new house'

SESSIONS FOR 7–8-YEAR-OLDS (YEAR 3)

6 You choose

Summary

Using the context of a quiz, this session asks pupils to reflect on how they could respond to challenges and take control.

Focus

Developing control

Outcome

To reflect on how we can control our responses to challenges

Resources

Teaching slides: Year 3 Session 6
Handout: You choose

Session

1. Arrange the pupils so they are sitting with a partner and able to see the board.
2. Reveal the word 'control' on the **first teaching slide** along with three possible definitions. Read the definitions through slowly and repeat this to ensure the pupils are clear on what they are. Then ask the pupils to reflect on: *What does the word 'control' mean?*

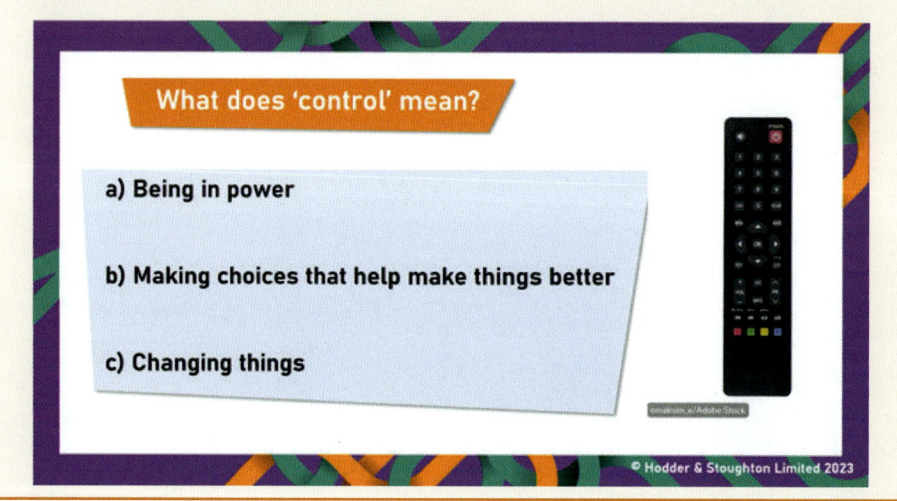

What does 'control' mean?

a) Being in power

b) Making choices that help make things better

c) Changing things

120

3. Provide the pupils with some talk time. The definitions have been written to stimulate discussion and to make the pupils think carefully about the meaning of control.
4. When the discussions have concluded, ask the pupils initially to respond with a show of hands to identify which they think is the best definition.
5. Develop this further by taking feedback from the pupils. At this point, pupils often respond by identifying that all three answers are about taking control.
6. Explain to the pupils that 'control' also means how they feel about being in control of their lives and their work: to think that they 'can do' things and that they can manage and control their emotions.
7. Explain to the pupils that they are going to be reflecting on how they can take control of challenges.
8. Reveal the first multiple-choice question on the **next teaching slide**. Read it carefully to the pupils and then allow them some time to discuss:
What would you do? Why?

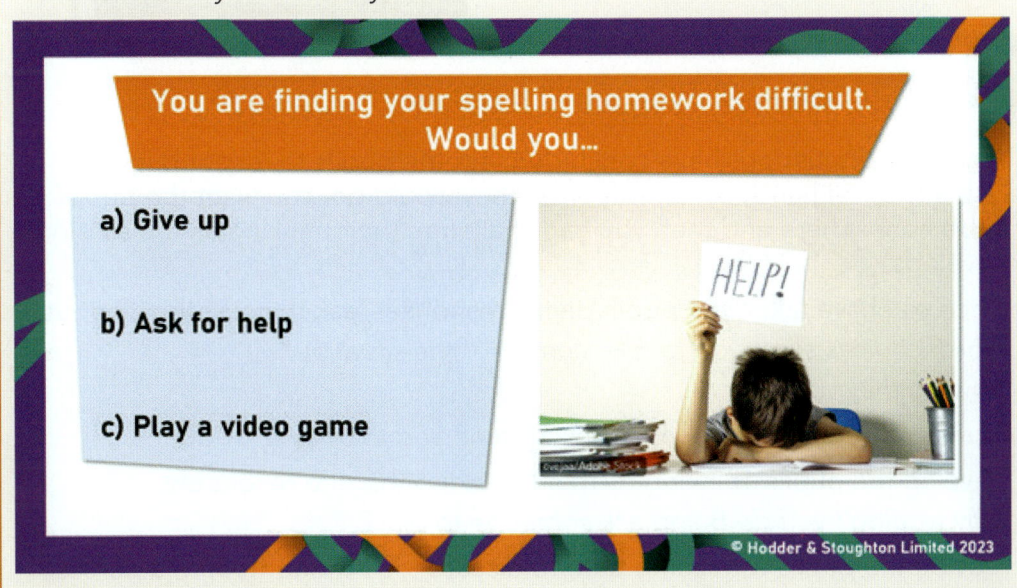

Multiple choice 1 – spelling

9. When the discussions have concluded, ask the pupils to respond initially with a show of hands to identify what they would do. You want the pupils to be honest here and then you can challenge their thinking as the session develops.
10. Develop this further by taking feedback from the pupils.
11. Explain to the pupils that asking for help takes control of the situation, whereas the other two just avoid doing something hard.

12 Reveal the second multiple-choice question on the **next teaching slide**. Read it carefully to the pupils and then allow them some time to discuss:
What would you do? Why?

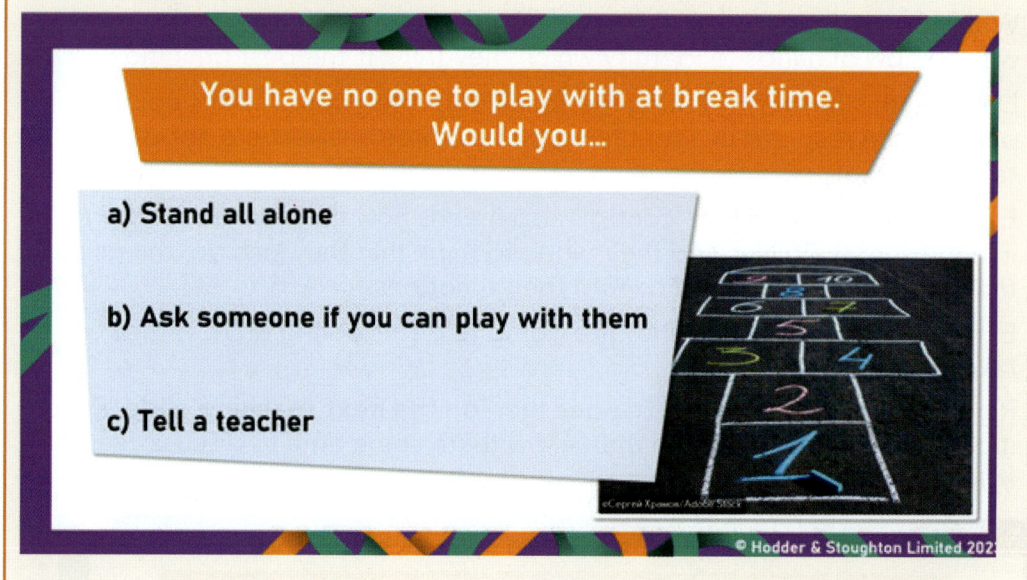

> **You have no one to play with at break time. Would you…**
>
> a) Stand all alone
>
> b) Ask someone if you can play with them
>
> c) Tell a teacher

Multiple choice 2 – Break time

13 When the discussions have concluded, ask the pupils to respond initially with a show of hands to identify what they would do. You want the pupils to be honest here and then you can challenge their thinking as the session develops.

14 Once you have taken the pupils' initial responses, ask them to think about:
Which choices allow you to take control of the situation?
How do they do this?

15 Provide the pupils with some thinking time and then take feedback.

16 Develop the pupils' thinking further by asking them to reflect on:
Why wouldn't you do B and ask someone to play?

17 Provide the pupils with some time to discuss their thoughts with a partner and then collect their ideas.

18 Reinforce the idea that taking control and doing something to improve a problem is much better than just reacting to it.

19 Reveal the third multiple-choice question on the **next teaching slide**. Read it carefully to the pupils and then allow them some time to discuss: *What would you do? Why?*

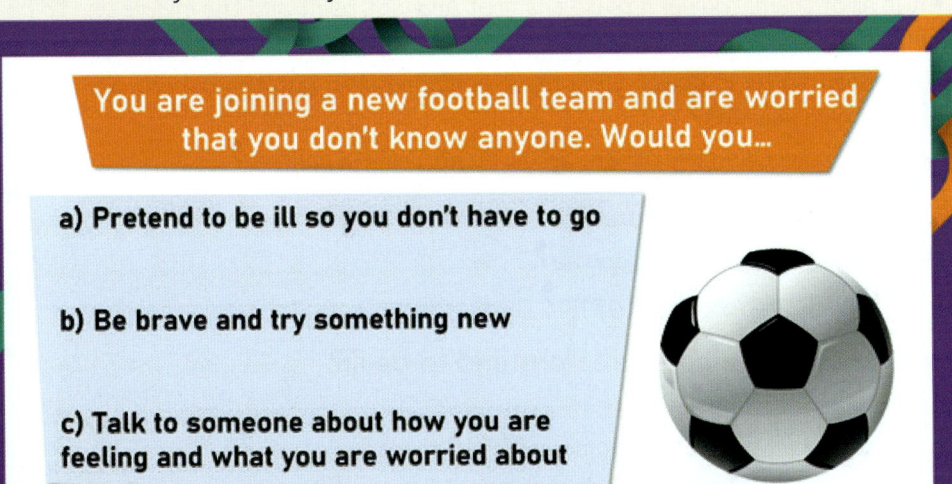

> **You are joining a new football team and are worried that you don't know anyone. Would you…**
>
> a) Pretend to be ill so you don't have to go
>
> b) Be brave and try something new
>
> c) Talk to someone about how you are feeling and what you are worried about

Multiple choice 3 – Football team

20 When the discussions have concluded, ask the pupils to respond initially with a show of hands to identify what they would do.

21 Once you have taken the pupils' initial responses, ask them to think about:
Which choices allow you to take control of the situation?
How do they do this?

22 Provide the pupils with some thinking time and then take feedback.

23 Develop the pupils' thinking further by asking them to reflect on:
Why would someone choose to pretend to be ill?

24 Provide the pupils with some time to discuss their thoughts with a partner and then collect their ideas.

25 Reinforce the idea that taking control and doing something to improve a problem is much better than just reacting to it.

Follow up

Pupils can create their own quiz with a problem and possible responses, using the **handout**. They should include two responses which enable them to take control and one that is a reaction.

SESSIONS FOR 7–8-YEAR-OLDS (YEAR 3)

> **Pupils' responses**
>
> What does 'control' mean?
> > 'It is all of them. You need to do the first and last point and the middle one to be in control.'
> >
> > 'You need to be in power to control someone else, but the others are about controlling yourself.'
> >
> > 'Being in power, and the others are all about being in control.'
>
> Why wouldn't you do B and ask someone to play?
> > 'As you are scared, they'd say no.'
> >
> > 'You want to play your own game.'
>
> Why would someone choose to pretend to be ill?
> > 'As you are nervous.'
> >
> > 'You might be worried that someone might make fun of you.'
>
> Your going bowling with your brownies and your worried that you will lose
>
> which one will you choose?....
>
> A. Tell your parents the song they to go
>
> B. Try your best to do it
>
> C. Tell your friend how your feeling

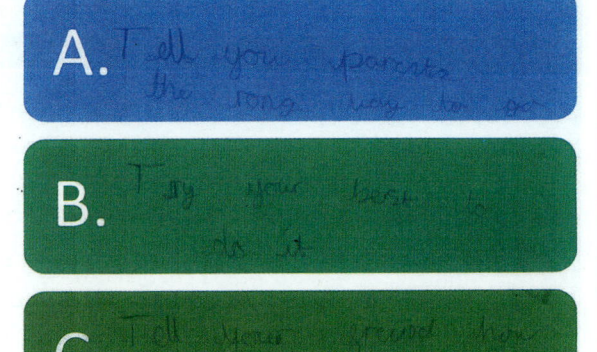

6 You choose

You are starting a new school and don't have any friends or BFR BFFS. What would u do?

A. ☺ try to make friends.
B. ☺☑ talk to a teacher
C. St── ou─ of sight.

You can't concentrate in class. Would you...

A. Be Silly
B. Shout out
C. Tell some one
D. Try Hard

Pupils' responses to 'You choose'

SESSIONS FOR 7–8-YEAR-OLDS (YEAR 3)

7 Erupting

Summary

Using the image of a volcano, this session reflects on how our behaviours and emotions can overwhelm us.

Focus

Developing control

Outcome

To explore how we can control our reactions

Resources

Clip of volcano erupting
Teaching slides: Year 3 Session 7
Handout: Erupting volcano alternative responses

Session

1. Arrange the pupils so they are sitting with a partner and can see the board clearly.
2. Share with the pupils the clip of a volcano erupting, following the link on the **first teaching slide**. Explain to them that they need to watch it carefully as you are going to ask them some questions about it.
3. Ask them to reflect on:
   What is happening?
   What did you notice?
4. Take feedback from the pupils on what they have seen, drawing out the ideas that it is exploding, firing hot lava and reacting strongly.
5. Explain to the pupils that you have shared this clip as we can all feel and behave like a volcano: that we can feel overwhelmed by our emotions, sometimes because we are anxious or worried or because we feel angry; that we can erupt and do and say things that we shouldn't or that don't help with a problem.

7 ERUPTING

6 Using the **next teaching slide**, share with the pupils the image of the erupting volcano that shows things the pupils might say or how they might behave.

Erupting volcano

7 Ask the pupils to reflect on:
   Have you ever felt or behaved like this?
   What happened?

8 Provide the pupils with some thinking time and then ask them to share their experiences with their talk partner.

9 Ask for volunteers to share their experiences.

10 Share the **handout** that shows the image of the erupting volcano and the behaviours and things that might get said when we erupt. This can be personalised to reflect behaviours that the pupils in your class demonstrate. Reinforce the idea that we all erupt and behave in different ways.

11 Focus the pupils on the image of the volcano and the things they might say or do when erupting. Review the different behaviours and things that could be said with the pupils and then ask them to reflect on:
   Are there any other things you do or say when you erupt?

12 Provide some talk time and then ask the pupils to share their ideas.

127

Sessions for 7–8-year-olds (Year 3)

> **13** Select one of the behaviours or things that might be said when we erupt and ask the pupils to think of different behaviours or things that might be said:
> *What should we do or say instead of saying 'I am rubbish'?*
>
> **14** Take feedback from the pupils on the alternative things that they could do or say.
>
> **15** Explain to the pupils that we are going to think positively and take control of the situation and stop ourselves from erupting. Ask them to record on the handout what they could do or say instead.
>
> **16** Provide the pupils with some time to record their ideas. They may wish to use an alternative colour pen to represent the positive.

Follow up

Create a class display containing visual prompts to reinforce the positive behaviours.

Pupils' responses

What is happening? What did you notice?
- *'It became very hot and smoke came out.'*
- *'It got darker.'*
- *'It was splashing about.'*
- *'The lava erupts.'*

Have you ever felt or behaved like this? What happened?
- *'I erupted as I was scared so I shouted for my dad and stayed still.'*
- *'I was excited to go somewhere but I found out it had been cancelled so I cried and cried. It all came out.'*

Are there any other things you do or say when you erupt?
- *'Wreck the house or make things messy.'*
- *'Break something.'*
- *'Tantrum.'*
- *'Scream into a cushion.'*
- *'Hurt someone.'*
- *'Scream.'*
- *'Remove yourself.'*

What should we do or say instead of saying 'I am rubbish'?
- *'You might not be able to do this straight away, but you need to think about the positives and what you can do.'*

7 ERUPTING

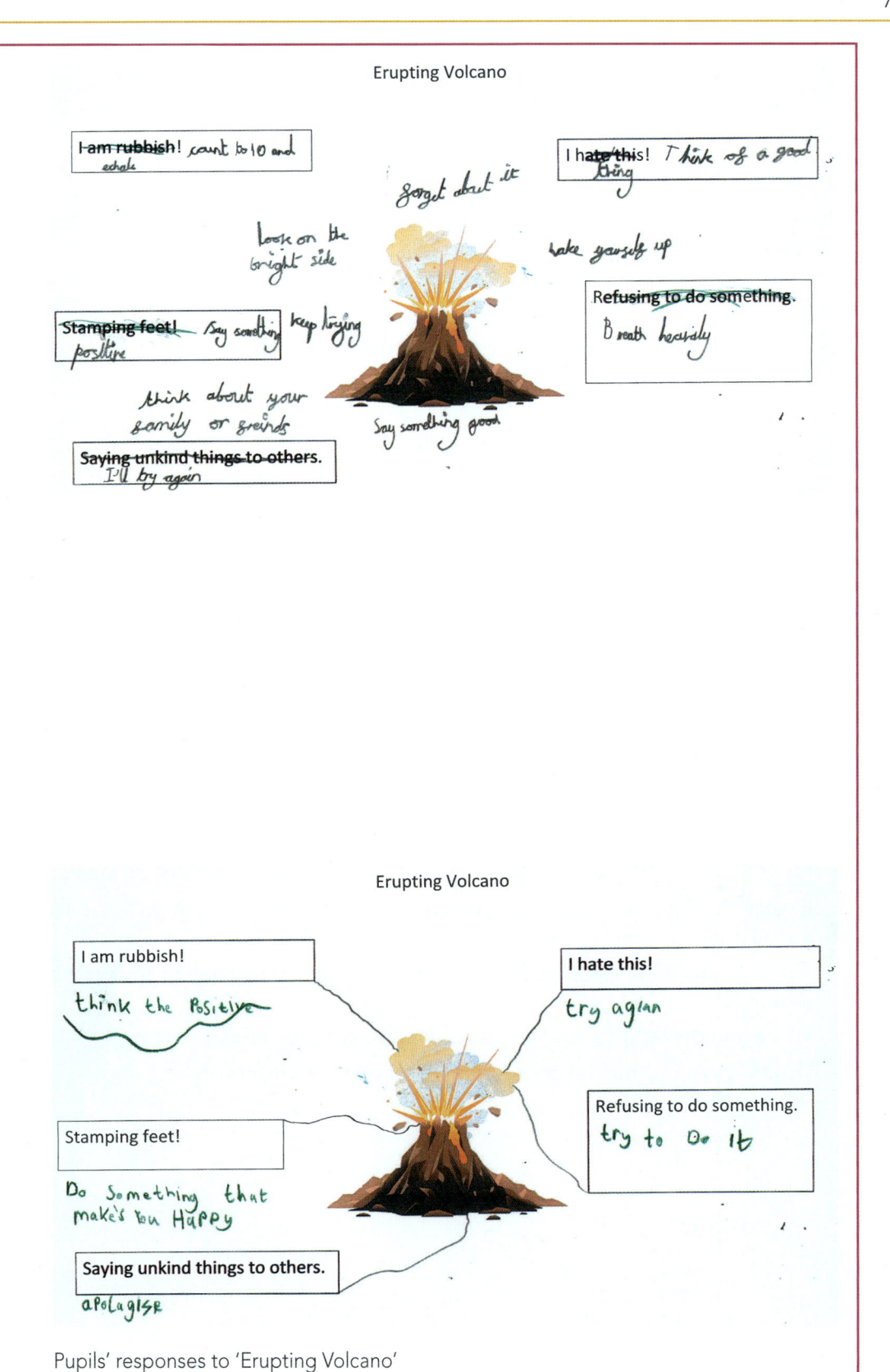

Erupting Volcano

- I am rubbish! count to 10 and exhale
- forget about it
- I hate this! Think of a good thing
- Look on the bright side
- wake yourself up
- Stamping feet! Say something positive
- keep trying
- Refusing to do something. Breath heavily
- think about your family or friends
- Say something good
- Saying unkind things to others. I'll try again

Erupting Volcano

- I am rubbish! — think the Positive
- I hate this! — try agian
- Stamping feet! — Do something that makes you Happy
- Refusing to do something. try to Do it
- Saying unkind things to others. apologise

Pupils' responses to 'Erupting Volcano'

8 Perfect recipe

Summary

Using the concept of a recipe, this session asks pupils to reflect on a personal challenge and to plan their approach.

Focus

Developing control, challenge, commitment and confidence

Outcome

To plan how we would approach a challenge

Resources

Teaching slides: Year 3 Session 8

Session

1. Arrange the pupils so they are sitting with a partner and can see the board.
2. Revisit the 4Cs with the pupils using the 4Cs poster or **first teaching slide**.
3. Share with the pupils the image of a recipe using the **next teaching slide**.
4. Ask the pupils to think about:
   What does a recipe need?
5. Provide the pupils with some time to think and then collect their ideas.
6. Explain to the pupils that you are going to focus on creating a recipe for a challenge.
7. Ask them to think about an area in which they wish to challenge themselves to improve:
   What do you want to challenge yourself to get better at?
8. You may wish to model an area in which you want to improve.

8 PERFECT RECIPE

> ### Visible Thinking
>
> 'I want to improve in my writing.'
> Provide them with some thinking time and then ask some pupils to share their potential challenges. You may need to encourage the pupils to be specific in their challenges, e.g. if they wish to improve in maths, encourage them to select a specific aspect.

9 Select one of the pupils' challenges to use as an example with the class, e.g. to learn my 8 times table.

10 Ask the pupils to think about this specific challenge and what you might need to do to achieve it.

11 Provide the pupils with some time to discuss their ideas and eavesdrop on their conversations.

12 Collect some of the pupils' ideas and record them on the board. The pupils will suggest both concrete ideas, such as a notebook, and more abstract ideas, such as resilience or commitment.

13 Develop the pupils' thinking further by asking them to break down into steps how they can get better at their 8 times tables.

14 Provide the pupils with some discussion time and then collect their ideas. Model the key steps as part of a recipe for success.

15 Revisit the key steps and ask the pupils to identify one step they can do towards their challenge.

Follow up

Pupils can write their recipe for how to be successful at their challenge.

Pupils' responses

What do you want to challenge yourself to get better at?

> *'To be more resilient.'*
> *'To learn my 8 times table.'*
> *'To get better at maths.'*

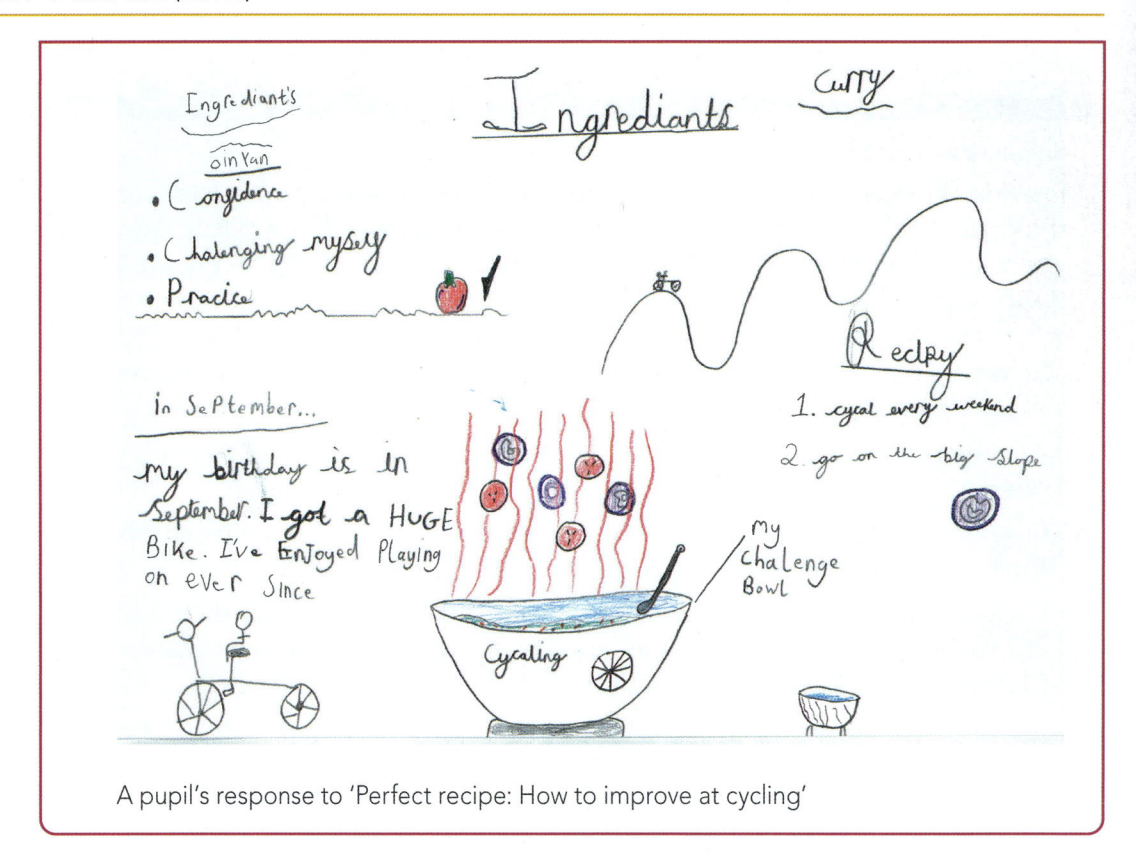

Sessions for 7–8-year-olds (Year 3)

A pupil's response to 'Perfect recipe: How to improve at cycling'

Sessions for 8–9-year-olds (Year 4)

Session	Focus	Outcomes	Summary	Page
1 My remote control – managing worries	Developing control	To identify how we feel when we are worried To identify aspects of our worries that we can control To identify strategies to help manage our worries	Introducing the idea of our inner remote control, this session explores control and how we can control our behaviours and manage difficult situations.	136
2 Dominoes of learning	Developing control and challenge	To reflect on what is needed to be successful at a task To identify how we need to break tasks into smaller steps	Using the image of a dominoes rally, this session reflects on how we can break challenges into smaller manageable steps that together enable us to achieve our goals.	139

Sessions for 8–9-year-olds (Year 4)

Session	Focus	Outcomes	Summary	Page
3 I am awesome	Developing confidence	To identify something that you are successful at To reflect on what makes us successful	This session asks pupils to reflect on their strengths and achievements, and encourages them to reflect on why they have been successful. (For some pupils, this will be a challenging session as they will not feel comfortable identifying positive things about themselves.)	142
4 Tough guys	Developing control, challenge and confidence	To identify characteristics of stereotypes To challenge preconceptions of what makes us 'tough'	This session explores our preconceptions about stereotypes and delves deeper into what makes us 'tough', using the 4Cs.	146
5 Building our inner strength	Developing control and confidence	To describe how we feel when things go wrong To reflect on how mistakes and challenges help us to build our mental strength	This session asks pupils to reflect on how responding to and coping with setbacks helps to build our mental strength. (It explores how dealing with our emotions and moving forward helps to build our resilience and leads to success.)	150

Session	Focus	Outcomes	Summary	Page
6 Committed to …	Developing commitment	To identify different ways in which we show commitment to a task To explore different levels of commitment	Using a range of scenarios, this session explores the different ways in which we show commitment. It explores how we can develop our commitment and overcome obstacles.	154
7 Comfort zone	Developing challenge, commitment and confidence	To reflect on how we feel and behave when we are in our comfort zone or challenge zone To identify areas of learning where we operate in our comfort zone or challenge zone	This session explores the different zones of learning and how we feel when we are in our comfort zone and when we are being challenged. Pupils will reflect on themselves as learners and identify behaviours they display depending on the zone in which they are operating.	158
8 My wish	Developing control, challenge, commitment and confidence	To identify an area in which they wish to improve To visualise what success (in this area) would look like	This session explores how to set clear goals and break these down into achievable steps. It asks pupils to reflect on potential barriers and how these can be overcome.	162

Overview

In Year 4, the elements of the 4Cs are explored in greater depth. Using specific contexts, pupils are encouraged to reflect on their own experiences and that of others. The sessions continue to normalise our initial responses to challenges and encourage pupils to develop strategies and mechanisms to overcome potential barriers. Pupils begin to visualise themselves being successful and explore how the 4Cs can help them to achieve their goals.

SESSIONS FOR 8–9-YEAR-OLDS (YEAR 4)

1 My remote control – managing worries

Summary

Introducing the idea of our inner remote control, this session explores control and how we can control our behaviours and manage difficult situations.

Focus

Developing control

Outcome

To identify how we feel when we are worried
To identify aspects of our worries that we can control
To identify strategies to help manage our worries

Resources

Teaching slides: Year 4 Session 1
Handout: Isaam and maths scenario

Session

1. Reveal the word 'control' on the **first teaching slide** and ask the pupils to discuss with their talk partner:

   What does the word 'control' mean?

   Explain to the pupils that there are no right or wrong answers and that you are just interested in hearing their opinions.

   ### Visible Thinking

   Control refers to developing our control of how we respond to challenges, how we react and how we create solutions to overcome difficulties, using our inner remote control.

2. Ask the pupils for feedback on their thoughts. During the feedback, you could ask the other pupils to listen carefully and think about whether they agree with others' ideas. Pupils can indicate their responses by an action, e.g. hands apart if they disagree and hands together if they agree. The use of this strategy ensures that they are active listeners.

1 My remote control – managing worries

3. Develop the discussion further by posing the question:
   How do we feel and behave when we are worried and don't feel in control?
   You may ask the pupils to respond by answering the question or demonstrating how they might behave: tell me, show me. Listen carefully to the discussions and then ask pupils for feedback on their thoughts.

4. Share with the pupils the image of a remote control on the **next teaching slide**. Ask the pupils:
   What do you use this for?
   How do you feel when you have it?
   Take feedback from the pupils.

5. Explain to the pupils that we all have an inner remote control that helps us manage our emotions, our reactions and our behaviours. Explain that having this 'remote control' means that we can change things, that we have choices about how we behave, think and react.

6. Share the scenario below with the pupils using the **next teaching slide** and the **handout**.

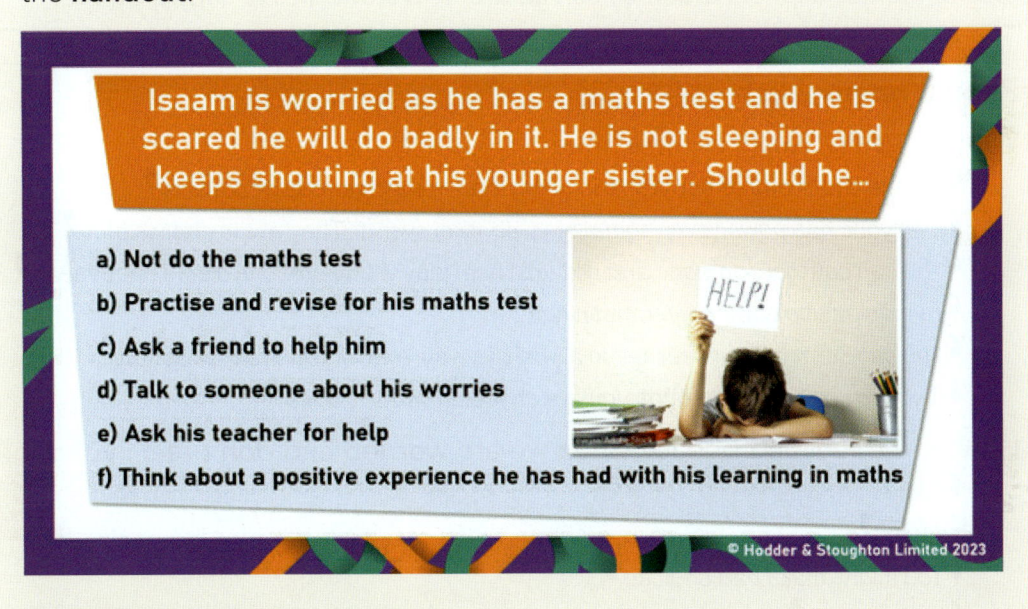

> Isaam is worried as he has a maths test and he is scared he will do badly in it. He is not sleeping and keeps shouting at his younger sister. Should he…
>
> a) Not do the maths test
> b) Practise and revise for his maths test
> c) Ask a friend to help him
> d) Talk to someone about his worries
> e) Ask his teacher for help
> f) Think about a positive experience he has had with his learning in maths
>
> © Hodder & Stoughton Limited 2023

Isaam and the maths test scenario

7. Ask the pupils to work with a talk partner and to think about our 'inner remote control' to identify the things that Isaam can control and change in the situation and the ones he can't. Ask them to sort them into groups and think carefully about why they think he can control them.

8. Once the discussions are underway, eavesdrop on the pupils as their discussions will be very illuminating. Then select a pair to share their initial thoughts.

9. Remind the pupils that, during the feedback, they should listen carefully and think about whether they agree with the ideas and sorting. Pupils can indicate their responses by an action, e.g. hands apart if they disagree and hands together if they agree. The use of this strategy ensures that they are active listeners.

10. You may wish to develop the discussions further by focusing on one of the pupils' responses and asking the pupils to reflect more specifically on what other elements they can control. Ask the pupils:
    Are there any other aspects of this situation that Isaam could control?
    Can you suggest ways in which he could control …?

Follow up

The pupils could create their own situation and aspects that could be controlled for their peers to support. You could generate real-life worries for your class to reflect on and identify aspects that they can control and strategies to support them.

Pupils' responses

What does the word 'control' mean?
- *Means if it is out of control it is going mad like a tiger out of control.*
- *Everyone has power over something, control over it. They are in charge of it.*
- *You can control someone and not let them play with someone else. That's mean.*
- *To manipulate someone/something.*
- *You can control your feelings in a positive way, even if you are feeling bad.*
- *If you're controlling a robot you are choosing what it does.*

How do we feel and behave when we are worried and don't feel in control?
- *Sad.*
- *Angry.*
- *You might make bad choices.*
- *Feel useless.*
- *Someone might have to help you control things.*
- *Cry and be upset.*

Isaam's scenario
- *Asking a friend to help could stop you worrying.*
- *You can control things by thinking about a positive experience, as a distraction and it would cheer you up.*
- *Talking to someone can help if you're worried. But just saying 'it is fine' doesn't help. It doesn't make your worry feel important.*
- *You still have to do the test; you need to control how you get ready for it.*

2 Dominoes of learning

Summary

Using the image of a dominoes rally, this session reflects on how we can break challenges into smaller manageable steps that together enable us to achieve our goals.

Focus

Developing control and challenge

Outcome

To reflect on what is needed to be successful at a task

To identify how we need to break tasks into smaller steps

Resources

Teaching slides: Year 4 Session 2

Dominoes

Handout: Dominoes of learning

Session

1. Arrange the pupils so they are sitting with a talk partner and can see the board.
2. Share with the pupils the image of the dominoes on the **teaching slide**.

Then ask them:
What happens?

3. Develop the pupils' thinking further by modelling how to build a dominoes rally badly. Leave large gaps between the dominoes and place them at different angles so they won't fall. Then ask the pupils:
What is going to happen?
Why?

SESSIONS FOR 8–9-YEAR-OLDS (YEAR 4)

4. Watch the clip of the dominoes rally by following the link on the **teaching slide**. Then ask the pupils to discuss with their partner:
   Why is it successful?
   Provide the pupils with some time to discuss their ideas with their partner and then take feedback.

5. Model connectivity using the dominoes – that when one domino falls, it knocks the next.

6. Explain to the pupils that the dominoes can represent all the challenges and things that we have to do; that once we start to do the first step it can then lead us to the next.

7. Explore with the pupils breaking down a challenging task into smaller steps, e.g. completing their maths homework. Share with the pupils the smaller manageable steps that they can break it down into:
   - Find somewhere quiet.
   - Gather your equipment.
   - Read the question.
   - Have a go.
   - Ask for help if you need it.
   - Record your answer.
   - Move on to the next question.

8. Remind the pupils, next time they have to do something, to think about the dominoes and try to knock one step down at a time.

Follow up

Explain to the pupils that, when we are facing challenges, we need to break them down into smaller steps that we can complete like knocking down the dominoes. Ask them to think about how to break a challenge down into smaller steps (dominoes). They could use the **handout** to do this.

Pupils' responses

What happens?

'All the dominoes were pushed over.'

'They followed on.'

'There was a pattern.'

Model building a dominoes rally badly: What is going to happen? Why?

'They are not close enough.'

'They won't impact on each other.'

'It's the wrong shape.'

'They are not in a line or close enough.'

2 DOMINOES OF LEARNING

Watch the clip: Why is it successful?

'They were all in the right place.'
'They went in the right direction.'
'They were on a flat and safe surface.'
'They are not too far away or too close.'
'They were lined up correctly.'

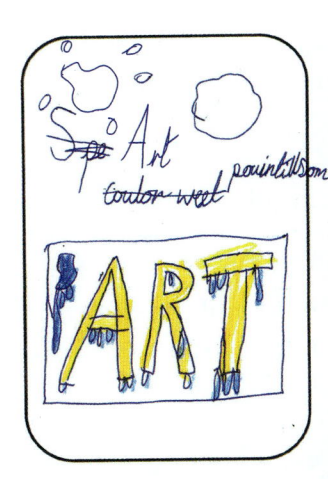

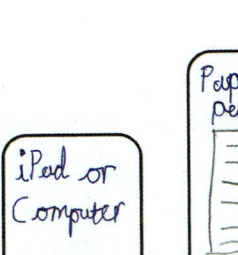

Pupils' responses to 'Dominoes of learning'

Sessions for 8–9-year-olds (Year 4)

3 I am awesome

Summary

This session asks pupils to reflect on their strengths and achievements, and encourages them to reflect on why they have been successful. (For some pupils, this will be a challenging session as they will not feel comfortable identifying positive things about themselves.)

Focus

Developing confidence

Outcome

To identify something that you are successful at
To reflect on what makes us successful

Resources

Teaching slides: Year 4 Session 3
Handout: I am awesome

Session

1. Arrange the pupils so they are sitting with a talk partner and can see the board clearly.
2. Reveal the phrase 'You're awesome' on the **first teaching slide** and ask the pupils to discuss with their partner:
   What does 'You're awesome' mean?
3. Provide the pupils with some talk time and then take feedback. If there is another member of staff available, they could act as a scribe to collect the pupils' initial ideas on the board. During the discussions, you want to elicit that 'being awesome' is something positive, that it is a compliment, and that there are many different reasons why a person might be 'awesome'.

Visible Thinking

During this session you want to encourage the pupils to think positively about themselves and others by identifying why they are awesome. If the only feedback we provide is that someone is awesome, then this does not help develop a healthy self-esteem; instead, it provides empty feedback and reinforces the notion that you always need praise when you do something, which can limit learning. Instead, we want to praise specifically the aspects they have learnt to be good at or their individual characteristics that make them effective, e.g. being a good listener or being kind.

4. Ask the pupils:

   What does 'awesome' mean?

   Develop the pupils' thinking further by asking them to think of synonyms for the word:

   What is a synonym for 'awesome'?

   Take feedback from the pupils and collect their ideas on the board so they can be referred to later or during other sessions.

5. Explain to the pupils that often we don't find it easy to identify things that we are good at. We can feel like we are bragging or showing off and we feel uncomfortable doing this. Everyone has days when they find it hard to identify something they are good at as some days we can feel like we are not good at anything.

6. Ask the pupils:

   What are you awesome at?

   Give them some thinking time. Ask the pupils to show you that they are ready to share by showing a thumbs-up and then select some pupils to share what they believe they are awesome at.

7. Some pupils may find this activity quite challenging and may need support from an adult at identifying what they are awesome at. You may also be given responses such as 'I am rubbish at everything'. Comments such as this need to be challenged and reframed by adults. It is important that you identify something that you believe the pupil to be 'awesome' at.

8. Display the **next teaching slide** and explain to the pupils that you have been reflecting on what makes you awesome at being a teacher, and then share the skills and attributes that have helped you to become awesome at teaching. These could include:
   - being good at listening
   - working hard
   - preparing and researching the subjects that you teach
   - being kind.

I am awesome at teaching because…
- I am a good listener
- I work hard
- I spend time preparing and researching the subjects that I teach
- I am kind

SESSIONS FOR 8–9-YEAR-OLDS (YEAR 4)

> 9 Explain to the pupils that these are the invisible things that have enabled you to learn and become an awesome teacher.
> 10 Ask the pupils:
> *What invisible things and behaviours help you to be awesome at …?*
> 11 Provide them with some time to record their ideas on the **handout.**

Follow up

Create a class display sharing what the pupils and staff are awesome at and the invisible skills that have helped them to achieve this.

Pupils' responses

What does 'You're awesome' mean?
- 'You have a good personality; you're determined and don't give up.'
- 'It's a compliment.'
- 'If you're awesome you could be talented and do something other people can't!'
- 'You're cool and great.'

What does 'awesome' mean?
- 'Something good.'
- 'Different way of saying I like something.'
- 'It's the opposite of uncool.'
- 'It's a more powerful word than good.'

What is a synonym for 'awesome'?
- 'Amazing'
- 'Fantastic'
- 'Cool'
- 'Great'
- 'Brilliant'
- 'Wonderful'

What are you awesome at?
- 'I am awesome at making people laugh.'
- 'I am awesome at maths.'
- 'I am awesome at football.'
- 'I am awesome at swimming.'
- 'I am awesome at being a good friend.'
- 'I am awesome at gymnastics.'

3 I AM AWESOME

What invisible skills and behaviours help you to be awesome at …?

- I AM AWESOME AT DRAWING
- I watch videos
- I good Progress better better
- I have a book which helps me
- I enjoy it
- My Parents think I'm good at it as well!

I am awesome

A pupil's response to 'I am awesome'

4 Tough guys

Summary

This session explores our preconceptions about stereotypes and delves deeper into what makes us 'tough', using the 4Cs.

Focus

Developing control, challenge and confidence

Outcomes

To identify characteristics of stereotypes

To challenge preconceptions of what makes us 'tough'

Resources

Teaching slides: Year 4 Session 4

Tough Guys (Have Feelings Too) by Keith Negley (2019)

Visualiser

Session

1. Arrange the pupils so they are sitting with a partner and able to see you and the board clearly.
2. Share with the pupils the front cover of the book *Tough Guys (Have Feelings Too)* by Keith Negley. Ask the pupils to discuss with their talk partners:
   How do you think a 'tough guy' behaves?
   Explain to the pupils that there are no right or wrong answers and that you are just interested in their different opinions.
3. Provide the pupils with some time for their discussions and then take feedback. Develop the discussion further by asking:
   What do tough guys look like?
   Are only guys tough?
4. Explain to the pupils that they are going to be detectives and they need to look carefully at the illustrations as they will be telling a story.
5. Read the book *Tough Guys (Have Feelings Too)* by Keith Negley. Pause after page 10 and ask the pupils to share:
   What did you notice?
   What did you see in the illustrations?
   To support the discussions, you may wish to use a visualiser to enable the pupils to look closely and zoom in on the illustrations.

6 Take feedback from the pupils and then develop the discussions further by asking them to reflect on:

Does the book match with your initial thoughts about tough guys?
How is it different?
Why do you think that is?

Again, provide the pupils with some talk time to deepen their discussions. You may wish to eavesdrop on their discussions and then share some of their key ideas, including misconceptions, during feedback, e.g. if a pupil suggests that the book is wrong and tough guys don't have anyworries, you can explore this further. You may wish to ask the pupils to state whether they agree or disagree with the statement and then allow them to share their opinions and their reasoning.

7 Share with the pupils the image of the superheroes on the **teaching slide** and ask them to reflect on:

What should being 'tough' look like?
How should we behave?
What should we say?

Take feedback from the pupils and then develop their thinking further by exploring 'being tough' as a learner.

8 Explain to the pupils that we can use the 4Cs to demonstrate how we can behave when we need to show our mental toughness and strength. Explain how the different elements enable us to be strong and help us to learn.

CONTROL	CHALLENGE
Developing our control of how we respond to challenges, how we react and how we create solutions to overcome difficulties. Using our inner remote control.	Wanting to challenge ourselves and trying new challenges to help ourselves grow.
COMMITMENT	**CONFIDENCE**
Sticking at something even when it is tricky and being resilient helps us to grow.	Identifying what we are good at and recognising this is important.

> **Follow up**
>
> A display could be created that shows the 4C behaviours and what we would say if we were demonstrating our mental strength.
>
> Pupils could be asked to reflect on characters in books, in films and on television, and to analyse their mental strength, collecting examples of how and when they demonstrate it.

Pupils' responses

How do you think a 'tough guy' behaves?
- 'They can be annoying.'
- 'They are good and help people.'
- 'They act like they know everything.'
- 'They act tough on the outside as they don't want people to know they are soft on the inside.'
- 'They brag about being strong.'

What do tough guys look like?
- 'Big biceps.'
- 'Muscles.'
- 'Not all tough guys have muscles.'
- 'Tall.'
- 'Strong.'

Are only guys tough?
- 'No – because some worked hard to be strong and tough.'
- 'Anyone can be strong if they put their mind to it. Physically strong and strong inside.'
- 'No, you can be tough by not minding what people say.'

What did you notice? What did you see in the illustrations?
- 'All of the tough guys look sad.'
- 'They were all men.'
- 'The astronaut had a picture of someone he missed in his hand.'

Does the book match with our initial thoughts about tough guys? How is it different? Why do you think that is?
- 'No, I thought it would have a happy start to it.'
- 'The tough guys are sad, and you don't expect that.'
- 'It is trying to show you that everyone finds challenging things hard.'

What should being 'tough' look like? How should we behave? What should we say?

> 'It looks like the picture – being strong and powerful.'
>
> 'It is about being kind and helping people.'
>
> 'It is about standing up for yourself.'
>
> 'Not giving up and believing in yourself.'
>
> 'Being courageous.'
>
> 'Keeping trying when things have gone wrong.'
>
> 'We should say kind things and encourage others.'

SESSIONS FOR 8–9-YEAR-OLDS (YEAR 4)

5 Building our inner strength

Summary

This session asks pupils to reflect on how responding to and coping with setbacks helps to build our mental strength. (It explores how dealing with our emotions and moving forward helps to build our resilience and leads to success.)

Focus

Developing control and confidence

Outcomes

To describe how we feel when things go wrong

To reflect on how mistakes and challenges help us to build our mental strength

Resources

Teaching slides: Year 4 Session 5

Session

1. Arrange the pupils so they are sitting with a partner and can see the board.
2. During this session you need to collect the pupils' responses to share later in the session with the class. You may wish to ask another member of staff or a pupil to act as a scribe and collect them on the board.
3. Recap on the 4Cs using the poster or the **first teaching slide**. Revisit the different behaviours we would see if we were being effective at developing control, rising to challenges, being committed and growing in confidence.

CONTROL
Developing our control of how we respond to challenges, how we react and how we create solutions to overcome difficulties. Using our inner remote control.

CHALLENGE
Wanting to challenge ourselves and trying new challenges to help ourselves grow.

COMMITMENT
Sticking at something even when it is tricky and being resilient helps us to grow.

CONFIDENCE
Identifying what we are good at and recognising this is important.

5 BUILDING OUR INNER STRENGTH

4 Using the **next teaching slide**, share with the pupils an image of a scenario where something goes wrong – a spilt glass of water. You could personalise this session by using photographs of yourself dealing with different problems.

5 Begin by asking the pupils:
What has happened?
Then ask the pupils to discuss with their talk partner:
How would you feel if this happened to you?
Why would you feel like that?

6 Then, using the **next teaching slide**, share an image of a mistake:

7 Begin by asking the pupils:
What has happened?
Then ask the pupils to discuss with their talk partner:
How would you feel if this happened to you?
Why would you feel like that?

SESSIONS FOR 8–9-YEAR-OLDS (YEAR 4)

8 Repeat this activity using the image of a child falling off a bike (on the **next teaching slide**) which allows you to explore mistakes and failures in a real-life context.

9 Ask the pupils:
What has happened?
Then ask the pupils to discuss with their talk partner:
How would you feel if this happened to you?
Why would you feel like that?

10 Share with the pupils the words that have been collected on the board during the discussions. Ask them to reflect on:
What do you notice about these words?
How are the words connected?
Provide the pupils with some time to discuss their ideas with their partner and then take feedback.

11 Explain the following to the pupils:

Visible Thinking

These experiences and the mistakes that we make help build our mental strength. It can be challenging when things go wrong. When we spill water, we mop it up. When we fall off our bike, we get back up and try again. Every time we get back up, we build our resilience and we take control. It is okay to be on the floor or to be unhappy, but we have to get up. The process of getting back up makes us stronger.

Follow up

Refer to the words that have been collected and then create a list of antonyms that we should use instead. You could also collect the language around the 4Cs that helps encourage pupils to build resilience.

Ask the pupils to collect other scenarios that could stimulate discussions on how we can use the 4Cs to support us when we make mistakes or things go wrong.

Pupils' responses

Scenario 1: What has happened?
- 'You've spilt a glass of water.'
- 'Water has gone everywhere.'

How would you feel if this happened to you?
- 'Angry.'
- 'Upset.'
- 'Annoyed.'
- 'Embarrassed.'
- 'Frustrated.'
- 'Scared.'
- 'Worried – that you would get wet and get in trouble.'

Scenario 2: What has happened?
- 'You've made a mistake.'
- 'You are rubbing out a mistake.'

How would you feel if this happened to you?
- 'Panicking.'
- 'Embarrassed.'
- 'Scared.'
- 'Shocked.'
- 'Unimpressed.'
- 'Happy – as you can learn from it.'
- 'Worried – because you may get shouted at.'

Scenario 3: What has happened?
- 'Fallen off a bike.'
- 'Crashed.'

How would you feel if this happened to you?
- 'Hurt.'
- 'Nervous – especially if you fell off in front of people.'
- 'Sad – it might hurt.'
- 'Worried that you would get shouted at.'

How are the words connected?
- 'They are sad words.'
- 'Some of them mean the same.'
- 'Most of them are words about things that you don't want to happen.'
- 'The words are connected – they range from sad all the way to happy. You could put them in order. Most of the words would be nearer to sad.'

SESSIONS FOR 8–9-YEAR-OLDS (YEAR 4)

6 Committed to …

Summary

Using a range of scenarios, this session explores the different ways in which we show commitment. It explores how we can develop our commitment and overcome obstacles.

Focus

Developing commitment

Outcomes

To identify different ways in which we show commitment to a task

To explore different levels of commitment

Resources

Teaching slides: Year 4 Session 6
Handout: Commitment scenarios

Session

1. Arrange the pupils so they are sitting with a partner and can see the board.
2. Pose the question below and ask the pupils to discuss with their talk partner their initial thoughts. Explain that there are no wrong or right answers and that you are just interested in their opinions:
   What does the word 'commitment' mean?
3. Provide the pupils with some talk time and eavesdrop on their conversations. This will enable you to gather their definitions and identify any misconceptions.
4. Share with the class some of the pupils' initial definitions of commitment and, if there are any misconceptions, share these and provide additional talk time for the pupils to reflect on whether they think these are accurate. When you share the pupils' misconceptions, ensure that you do so anonymously to avoid any embarrassment. You can also reinforce the idea that we all make misconceptions by framing a misconception in a way that suggests that you also had this thought. The modelling of mistakes and misconceptions helps to normalise them.

5. Together, create a class definition of commitment, for example:

> ### 👁 Visible Thinking
>
> **Commitment** is sticking at something even when it is tricky and being resilient, which helps us to grow.
>
> Showing **commitment** means sticking at something that is difficult, even when it would be easier to give up; refusing to give up and finding ways to get better and overcome barriers until you are successful.

6. Develop the pupils' thinking further by asking them to reflect on:
   When have you shown commitment?
   Initially, you may wish to share your own example of when you have shown commitment to something. If you provide examples, ensure that you provide one that is based on learning and school and one that is outside of school. This reinforces the idea that we show commitment in different aspects of our lives. If the pupils only provide examples from outside of school, you may wish to ask them to reflect on showing commitment with their learning to focus their thinking further.

7. Provide the pupils with some thinking time and then select pupils to share examples. You may wish to develop their thinking further by asking them to reflect on their behaviour:
   How do you behave when you are committed to something?

8. Introduce the pupils to one of the commitment scenarios. Display the **first teaching slide** on the board and read it together.

> Jessica always tries her best; she finds maths challenging so she has been doing extra practise at home for her times tables and in class she has been asking the teacher for extra help.
>
> Micah likes to be first to finish and does his work very quickly. He does not like editing it to make it better.
>
> Amira keeps practicing her spellings as she wants to improve. She's asked her mum to help her and has asked her teacher how she should practise. She is still finding remembering them hard so is trying to find new ways of learning them. She refuses to give up.
>
> Fred knows he needs to get better at writing, when he has finished a piece, he tries to read it and check that he hasn't made any spelling mistakes.

Commitment scenarios

Ask the pupils to reflect on how the child has shown commitment. Ask them to think about:
How does ... show commitment?
How does he/she behave?

9 Provide the pupils with some talk time and then select pupils to share their opinions. To ensure all the pupils are active listeners you could ask them to listen carefully and, if they agree with the speakers' ideas, they should put their thumbs up. If they wish to add something to develop the discussion, they could indicate by touching their nose and, if they disagree, they can put their thumbs down.

10 Then provide the pupils with a range of different scenarios using the **handout** or use the rest of the **teaching slides**. Read them together and then ask the pupils initially to identify which scenarios contain someone displaying commitment.

11 Provide the pupils with some time to discuss the different scenarios and then take feedback from them. You may wish to challenge the discussions further by saying:

I think Micah is the most committed. What do you think?

Again, provide some talk time for the pupils to reflect on your viewpoint which should be the opposite of their thinking. This will encourage them to reflect on their opinions and provide evidence to justify them.

12 Develop the discussions further by posing the questions:

Who is the most committed?
Why?

Provide the pupils with some more time to discuss the scenarios. They may choose to rank them in order from the most committed to the least. Then take feedback. Ensure that you probe their thinking by asking them to justify their opinions.

Why do you think they are the most committed?
How do they behave?

Follow up

You could ask pupils to reflect and identify something to which they need to show further commitment. They could explore this with a partner in a mini coaching session. This would be particularly effective if staff members modelled a session beforehand and prompt cards were provided for the discussions, which could include:

What are you going to commit to?
How are you going to show further commitment?
How will you behave?
What will you do?

Pupils' responses

What does the word 'commitment' mean?
- 'You give everything to something, for example friendship.'
- 'Showing that you're not going to give up and you're committed.'
- 'It's like being loyal.'
- 'Giving your all to something.'
- 'If you commit to something – you are going to do it!'

When have you shown commitment?
- 'Trying to go down a scary slide.'
- 'With my homework – making myself do it and practising.'
- 'I am a fussy eater, but my mum put new things in my lunch, and I have committed to trying to eat them.'

How do you behave when you are committed to something?
- 'You may feel scared initially but when you've done it you are proud.'
- 'Determined – focused on it.'
- 'Ask for help.'
- 'Make time for it.'

I think Micah is the most committed. What do you think?
- 'No, if he's rushing it, he's not going to be successful.'
- 'Being fast doesn't mean it's good.'
- 'You need to do good work not fast work.'

Who is the most committed?

Jessica is the most committed. Why?
- 'Because she is being resilient as she keeps on trying.'
- 'Because she is asking for help and finds it hard.'
- 'She is trying lots of different things.'

Amira is the most committed. Why?
- 'Because she asks for extra help from the teacher, but Jessica doesn't.'
- 'She asks for extra help.'

What are you going to commit to?
- 'Neater handwriting.'
- 'Concentrating – even if I am sat next to my best friend.'
- 'Doing my best work – all of the time.'

SESSIONS FOR 8–9-YEAR-OLDS (YEAR 4)

7 Comfort zone

Summary

This session explores the different zones of learning and how we feel when we are in our comfort zone and when we are being challenged. Pupils will reflect on themselves as learners and identify behaviours they display, depending on the zone in which they are operating.

Focus

Developing challenge, commitment and confidence

Outcomes

To reflect on how we feel and behave when we are in our comfort zone or challenge zone

To identify areas of learning where we operate in our comfort zone or challenge zone

Resources

Teaching slides: Year 4 Session 7
Handout: Learning zones
Sticky notes

Session

1. Arrange the pupils so they are sitting with a talk partner and can see the board clearly.
2. Share the image of the different learning zones using the **teaching slide**.

3 Explain to the pupils the different zones of learning:

Visible Thinking

When we are learning something new, we move through different zones of learning. In the centre is our comfort zone. When we are operating in here, we are able to do the task easily. There is no element of challenge and we are confident in what we are doing. In the learning zone, we are receptive to new learning; we will find elements of it challenging and need to be committed to learning it, but we know we can learn it. Finally, there is the panic zone. This is when we can feel overwhelmed by new learning; we panic and don't believe that we can do it. Sometimes this may be due to missing knowledge or skills that we need prior to learning something new, or it can be because we are lacking confidence in ourselves.

4 Reinforce the explanation by sharing personal examples for the different zones, for example:

Visible Thinking

When I was learning to drive, at first, I felt in the panic zone. I was terrified and thought I would not be able to learn how to do it. I was scared that I would make mistakes. I made myself try and others encouraged me to believe in myself and I slowly moved into the learning zone. I had a good teacher and began to become more confident and learnt the skills and knowledge I needed. I passed my test and I had learnt how to drive. Now, I have the skills, knowledge and experience to drive a car and I am operating in my comfort zone.

5 Encourage the pupils to reflect on themselves as learners and pose the question:
What are you in your comfort zone for?

Provide the pupils with some time to reflect and then take feedback from them. If a pupil responds with an area that they are not in the comfort zone for or is too complex, such as playing football, ensure you clarify this and where it should be place in the learning zones.

6 Develop their thinking further by posing the questions:
What are you in the learning zone for?
What are you in the panic zone for?

Provide the pupils with the **handout** and some sticky notes on which they can record three different things that they are learning. They should stick each note onto the handout in the appropriate zone.

7 Ask for volunteers and share some examples of the pupils' handouts. Then pose the question:
How can we move something from the panic zone to the learning zone?

8 Provide the pupils with some time to talk to their partner and then develop their thinking further by asking:
How can the 4Cs help move something from the panic zone to the learning zone?

Sessions for 8–9-year-olds (Year 4)

> ### Follow up
> A class display of the learning zones could be created as a reference point for further discussions. It should include ways of moving yourself through the different zones and how this is linked to the 4Cs. The pupils should also revisit their own learning zones and move the aspects identified through the different zones, or add additional aspects related to current learning.

Pupils' responses

What are you in your comfort zone for?

- *Reading – because I love it and can do it!*
- *Cartwheels – because I have learnt how to do it and can do them instantly.*

What are you in the learning zone for?

- *Swimming – I know a lot. I can swim but I still have things to learn.*
- *Reading – I still find it hard and I need to practise.*
- *Horse-riding – I am in both the learning and sometimes the panic zone. I enjoy it but it can be stressful if it goes wrong.*

How can the 4Cs help move something from the panic zone to the learning zone?

- *Control – if you control your reactions and try not to worry it will help you improve and focus on the learning.*
- *Challenge – you have to like challenges and work towards them to move into the learning zone.*
- *If you are committed to getting better and work hard you can move through the zones.*
- *Confidence – if you have more confidence in yourself then you would move yourself out of the panic zone.*

7 Comfort zone

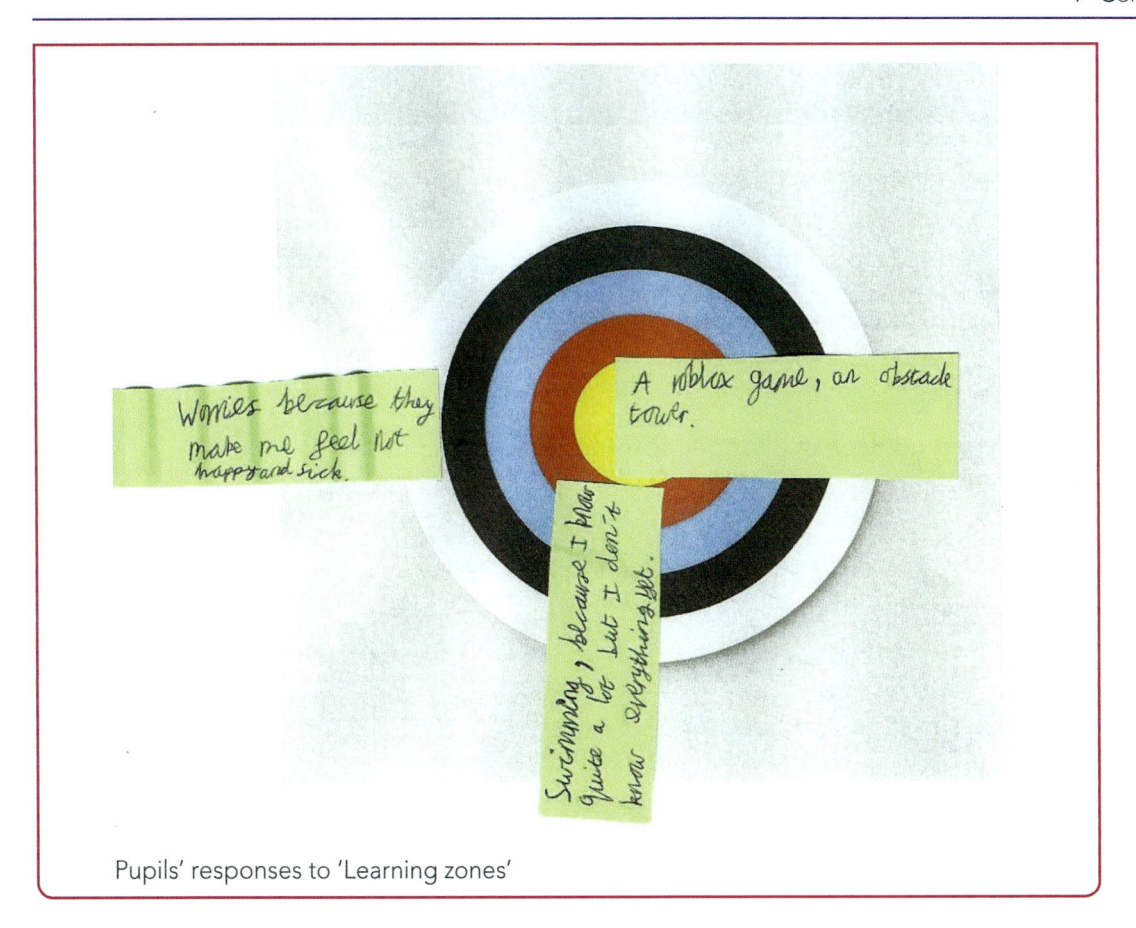

Pupils' responses to 'Learning zones'

8 My wish

Summary

This session explores how to set clear goals and break these down into achievable steps. It asks pupils to reflect on potential barriers and how these can be overcome.

Focus

Developing control, challenge, commitment and confidence

Outcomes

To identify an area in which they wish to improve

To visualise what success (in this area) would look like

Resources

Teaching slides: Year 4 Session 8
Handout: My wish

Session

1. Arrange the pupils so they are sitting with a partner and have a clear view of the images on the board.
2. Share the image of the genie's lamp using the **teaching slide** and ask the pupils:
   What does this image make you think of?
   Take some feedback from the pupils and then focus them on the concept of wishing.
3. Focus pupils' thinking further by asking them to spend a few minutes thinking in detail about something they want to get better at or learn how to do:
   What do you want to get better at?
   You may wish to focus their thinking on something relating to learning in school or a more personal choice. Do this through your questioning. Provide the pupils with some time to think and then select pupils to share their ideas. If there is a pupil who may be reluctant to share, talk to them during their thinking time and encourage them to share their thoughts.

4. Explain to the pupils that, once they have identified an area in which they wish to develop and improve, they then need to reflect on what being successful at this will look like. Encourage the pupils to create a successful vision for themselves that will help support them on their journey (along with breaking things down into manageable steps).

5. Take one of the pupils' examples and model what being successful at this would look like, e.g. writing a successful paragraph. You may wish to share these prompts on the board to focus the pupils' thinking:
What would being successful at this look like?
How would you feel if you were successful at your wish?

Visible Thinking

A successful paragraph will:
- include neat handwriting
- use interesting, high level vocabulary
- include good punctuation – used correctly
- use a range of sentences
- be relevant and detailed about the subject
- be engaging for the reader.

6. Ask the pupils to discuss what they would see if you were being successful at the area identified and create a list in a similar format to the example shared. The pupils may need some focused questioning to develop high-quality examples of success and some pupils may find this easier than others so you may need to scaffold support for them by providing choice:
Would a successful … include … or …?

7. Then provide the pupils with some time to create their own lists illustrating success in their chosen area. They could use the **handout** to do this. While they are completing these, move around the room and provide feedback and support where appropriate.

8. Finally, encourage the pupils to reflect on potential obstacles to their success. Provide pupils with the prompts to support their thinking:
What obstacles could get in your way?
How might you stop yourself from achieving the goal?
You may wish to model how you can self-sabotage your own success by thinking that you are not good enough and then stop trying. Encourage the pupils to think of potential solutions for this, e.g. if you get distracted easily – how can you prevent this?

Follow up

You may wish to split this session into two to enable deeper reflection by the pupils and more time to plan in detail.

Make time to revisit the pupils' plans for success and encourage them to identify each small step towards success.

You can use this visioning activity in other areas of the curriculum and life. Encourage the pupils to use the question prompts to support their thinking and reflection.

Pupils' responses

What do you want to get better at?

- 'Playing rugby.'
- 'Decimals.'
- 'Handwriting.'
- 'Cantering on a horse.'
- 'Writing paragraphs.'

How would you feel if you were successful at your wish?

- 'Happy.'
- 'Proud of myself.'
- 'Delighted.'

> I want to be better at football so I can play at a higher level

> Successfull if I am successfull I will enjoy it more

> If I get something wrong I might be cities 2nd might

A pupil's response to 'My Wish'

Sessions for 9–10-year-olds (Year 5)

Session title	Focus	Outcomes	Summary	Page
1 What I am thankful for …	Developing confidence	To identify aspects of their lives for which they are thankful	This session encourages pupils to reflect on what they are thankful for in their lives and the importance of taking time to acknowledge this.	167
2 Marshmallow test	Developing control and confidence	To explore the concepts of instant and delayed gratification To reflect on how they need to be rewarded in response to a task	This session introduces pupils to the idea of instant gratification and encourages them to reflect on how they respond to rewards.	170
3 Help me	Developing control and confidence	To reflect on why we should ask for help To identify ways in which we can help others	This session reinforces the idea that it is okay to ask for help and that we can all help each other and create a supportive community.	174
4 Stickability	Developing control, challenge, commitment and confidence	To identify how we can show stickability when completing a task	This session uses the context of problem solving to explore stickability and committing to a goal.	178

Sessions for 9–10-year-olds (Year 5)

Session title	Focus	Outcomes	Summary	Page
5 On track	Developing control, challenge, commitment and confidence	To identify an area in which they wish to challenge themselves To identify how they can break down their challenges into smaller steps	This session encourages pupils to identify an area in which they wish to challenge themselves. It uses visioning techniques to reinforce the steps to success and how we can break challenges down into achievable steps.	182
6 Network audit	Developing control and confidence	To create their own personal network audit	This session introduces the network audit, a simple tool that helps develop control and confidence. Pupils examine the people in their network and start to build a list of people that they can call upon in difficult times.	185
7 Just a minute	Developing control and commitment	To identify ways of overcoming procrastination	This session introduces pupils to the idea of procrastination and simple techniques to overcome it.	188
8 Agony Aunt	Developing control, challenge, commitment and confidence	To suggest solutions to problems To identify how they can use the 4Cs to approach problems	This session asks pupils to reflect on the 4Cs and how they can be applied to potential problems.	191

Overview

In Year 5, the sessions explore the 4Cs in wider contexts. Sessions link research to practical activities, exploring concepts including procrastinating, visioning and instant gratification. They explore collective efficacy and how the wider community can support the development of the 4Cs through network audits and problem solving.

1 What I am thankful for …

Summary

This session encourages pupils to reflect on what they are thankful for in their lives and the importance of taking time to acknowledge this.

Focus

Developing confidence

Outcome

To identify aspects of their lives for which they are thankful

Resources

Teaching slides: Year 5 Session 1
Handout: I am thankful for …

Session

1. Arrange the pupils so they are sitting with a partner and can see the board clearly.
2. Explain to the pupils that there are no right or wrong answers and that you are just interested in their opinions. Share with the pupils the word 'thankful' using the **teaching slide** and ask them to reflect on:
   What does the word 'thankful' mean?
3. Provide the pupils with some time to discuss their ideas with their partner and then take feedback from them.

Visible Thinking

Being **thankful** means expressing how happy and positive you are about something or someone, for example 'I am thankful for my brother as he helps me with my homework'.

4. Develop the pupils' thinking further by asking them:
   What is a synonym for 'thankful'?
5. Collect their ideas on the board. You may wish to develop their vocabulary further by modelling different words and using them in sentences. Explain:

Visible Thinking

We often focus on the negatives, the things we don't have and that we want, rather than on the things and the people that we do have. Taking time to reflect on what we are grateful for helps us to feel happier and more positive about our lives.

Sessions for 9–10-year-olds (Year 5)

6. Model some things that you are grateful for and explain the reasons why:

Visible Thinking

I am thankful for my daughter as she is very funny and makes me smile. I am thankful that I have learnt how to write and can transfer my ideas into books for teachers to use. I am thankful for my friends as they are always there for me and make me smile.

7. Ask the pupils to reflect on:
   What are you thankful for?
   Why?
8. Provide them with some thinking time and then ask for volunteers, or the whole class if you have time, to share what they are grateful for.
9. Explain to the pupils that we can be grateful for lots of different things: for people, objects, places, experiences, hobbies, things we have learnt how to do, our families and our communities.
10. Ask the pupils to reflect on four things they are thankful for and record them. Encourage them to categorise them and think about different things we can be thankful for, e.g. a person, an object, an experience and a community.
11. Pupils can record their ideas on the **handout**.

Follow up

You could have a thankful jar in the class, in which you collect a positive every day. The pupils could learn to spell positive words, e.g. gratitude. Together, reflect on the skills they are grateful for.

Pupils' responses

What does the word 'thankful' mean?

'Being really happy about something, for example, when someone gives you a present.'

'Being polite when someone has given you something.'

'It is about being grateful for what you've got.'

'Being appreciative.'

What is a synonym for 'thankful'?

'Grateful'

'Appreciative'

'Pleased'

'Satisfied'

1 What I am thankful for …

What are you thankful for?

I am thankful for ….

A pupil's response to 'I am thankful for …'

169

SESSIONS FOR 9–10-YEAR-OLDS (YEAR 5)

2 Marshmallow test

Summary

This session introduces pupils to the idea of instant gratification and encourages them to reflect on how they respond to rewards.

Focus

Developing control and confidence

Outcome

To explore the concepts of instant and delayed gratification

To reflect on how they need to be rewarded in response to a task

Resources

Teaching slides: Year 5 Session 2

Marshmallows

Handout: Instant and delayed gratification

Session

1. Arrange the pupils so they are sitting with a partner and can see the board and the marshmallows on the **first teaching slide**.

2. Present the pupils with two choices: a plate with one marshmallow on it and one with two. Explain to the pupils that they have a choice to make. They can either have one marshmallow now or they can wait ten minutes and have two marshmallows. You may wish to change the choice to something that is popular in the class such as chocolate or sweets.

3. Ask the pupils to think about:

   What would you choose to do? Why?

   Reiterate that they can only choose one option: instantly having one marshmallow or waiting and having two.

   Provide them with some thinking time and then ask them to discuss their choice with their talk partner. Encourage the pupils to explain why they made their choice.

4. During the discussions, eavesdrop on the pupils' conversations as this will reveal their preconceptions. Then ask pupils with different perceptions to share their opinions.
5. Explain to the pupils that the 'Marshmallow Experiment' was the first investigation into 'delayed gratification' and took place in the 1970s.

Visible Thinking

Explain to the pupils that **delayed gratification** means waiting longer for the reward/praise and not needing it instantly.

6. You may wish to watch the short film of the experiment being recreated – follow the link on the **first teaching slide.**

Visible Thinking

Explain to the pupils that **instant gratification** means that you are willing to forgo a future reward/benefit in order to receive a less rewarding benefit immediately. In this case, this involves getting only one marshmallow but getting it now rather than waiting a set amount of time to receive two.

7. Ask the pupils to reflect on their own experiences and how they feel about receiving instant gratification, e.g. when they receive positive feedback on a computer game.
   How do you feel about receiving instant gratification?
8. Provide the pupils with some time to discuss their ideas with their partner and then select some pupils to share their thoughts.
9. Develop the pupils' thinking further by asking them to reflect on the following statements and how they feel about them. Remind the pupils that we are all different and that our opinions and response will be unique.
10. Display the **next teaching slide** and share the **handout** with pupils. Ask the pupils to cut up the handout and give them time to sort the statements individually. You may wish to develop their thinking further by asking them to reflect on:
    Does the statement apply to you always, sometimes or never?

> - I like to be given instant feedback on my learning.
> - If I know that I have worked hard on something than I am proud of myself.
> - I enjoy playing computer games and being successful instantly.
> - If something is challenging, I will persevere.
> - I like doing things which are easy, and I can do quickly.
> - I enjoy doing something that is hard and that I can't do initially. I like to stick at it and keep trying.
> - I will do jobs at home if I get pocket money.
> - I like to help my family and do jobs at home.

11 Once the pupils have finished reflecting and have sorted the statements, ask them to share their thoughts with their talk partner.

12 During the discussions, ensure that you eavesdrop as this will highlight any preconceptions and misconceptions among the pupils which you may need to address later.

13 Explain to the pupils that the results of the experiment showed that the pupils who did not need instant gratification achieved more, e.g. better outcomes in tests.

14 Finally, ask the pupils to reflect on:
How can we delay our need for instant gratification?

Follow up

Ask the pupils to reflect on when they have demonstrated delayed gratification and create a mini-blog of different examples.

Pupils' responses

What would you choose to do? Why?

'Two marshmallows and waiting because I would do something else while I waited.'

'I would choose one marshmallow as it's not much more, so it won't make much difference.'

'One marshmallow as I don't like to wait.'

How do you feel about receiving instant gratification?

'Good because you don't have to wait.'

'Happy because I am pleased to get something.'

How can we delay our need for instant gratification?

'Get better at waiting.'

'Seeing work as long term.'

'Not focusing on it.'

'Put your mind on something else.'

'Think about the difference between what you get first and then what you get in the future.'

SESSIONS FOR 9–10-YEAR-OLDS (YEAR 5)

3 Help me

Summary

This session reinforces the idea that it is okay to ask for help and that we can all help each other and create a supportive community.

Focus

Developing control and confidence

Outcome

To reflect on why we should ask for help
To identify ways in which we can help others

Resources

Teaching slides: Year 5 Session 3

Sessions

1. Arrange the pupils so they are sitting with a partner and can see the board.
2. Share with the pupils the image of the girl asking for help on the **teaching slide** and ask them to discuss with their talk partner:
   Is it okay to ask for help?
   Why do you think that?

[Image: Illustration of a girl with a speech bubble saying "Can you help me?" on a yellow background. Credit: oushan/Adobe Stock. © Hodder & Stoughton Limited 2023]

3. Provide the pupils with some time to discuss their ideas and then select pupils to share their thoughts.

3 Help me

> **Visible Thinking** 👁
>
> Explain to the pupils that some people won't ask for help and think asking for help makes them look bad. However, at times we all need someone to help us and for lots of different reasons. We may need a friend to talk to if we are feeling sad, a teacher to help us with a spelling we are stuck on or someone to show us how we can do something.

4 Ask the pupils to reflect on:
   Can you remember a time when someone helped you?
   Provide some thinking time and then select pupils to share their own experiences.

5 Probe their thinking further by asking:
   How did you feel when you received help?
   What was the effect of the help you received?
   Allow the pupils some time to talk to their partner and 'eavesdrop' on their conversations and collect their thoughts.

6 Once the discussions have finished share some of the pupils' thoughts and then ask them to reflect on:
   When should we ask for help?

> **Visible Thinking** 👁
>
> Explain to the pupils that we all need help sometimes and share a personal experience of when someone has helped you and the impact it had.

7 Ask the pupils to think about their strengths and how they can use these to help others, e.g. if they have learnt how to pass a ball well in football or they can make great cakes or they know ways that help you learn spellings.

8 Ask the pupils to share how they can help each other in the classroom and develop their community. Create a class display sharing the different ways they can help each other as a point of reference for the pupils.

> **Follow up**
>
> Discuss different ways that the pupils can help themselves for different scenarios, e.g. stuck on a calculation in maths or what to do if you have fallen out with a friend.
>
> Create visual prompts to display in the classroom on how they can help themselves and others.

Pupils' responses

Is it okay to ask for help? Why do you think that?

> 'Yes – if you need it.'

> 'Not in a test!'

> 'Yes – because if you are stuck you could be stuck for a while.'

> 'It depends, if you are in an important test then no but if it's not important then yes.'

> 'It's okay to ask for help and ask for someone to show you how.'

Can you remember a time when someone helped you?

How did you feel when you received help?

What was the effect of the help you received?

> 'I couldn't open a parcel, so my mum helped me. The parcel got opened quicker with her help.'

> 'When I was little my mum used to help me undo my building blocks.'

> 'When I fell over, my friend helped me up.'

> 'When you can't do something, the teacher helps you. It makes me feel happier, better. I feel thankful.'

When should we ask for help?

> 'When you have tried yourself first.'

> 'When you are still learning.'

> 'You need to try yourself first.'

'I can help you' display

3 Help me

Pupils' responses to 'I can help you'

SESSIONS FOR 9–10-YEAR-OLDS (YEAR 5)

4 Stickability

Summary

This session uses the context of problem solving to explore stickability and committing to a goal.

Focus

Developing control, challenge, commitment and confidence

Outcome

To identify how we can show stickability when completing a task

Resources

Teaching slides: Year 5 Session 4

Session

1. Arrange the pupils so they can see the board.
2. Share with the pupils the three different shapes on the **first teaching slide**.

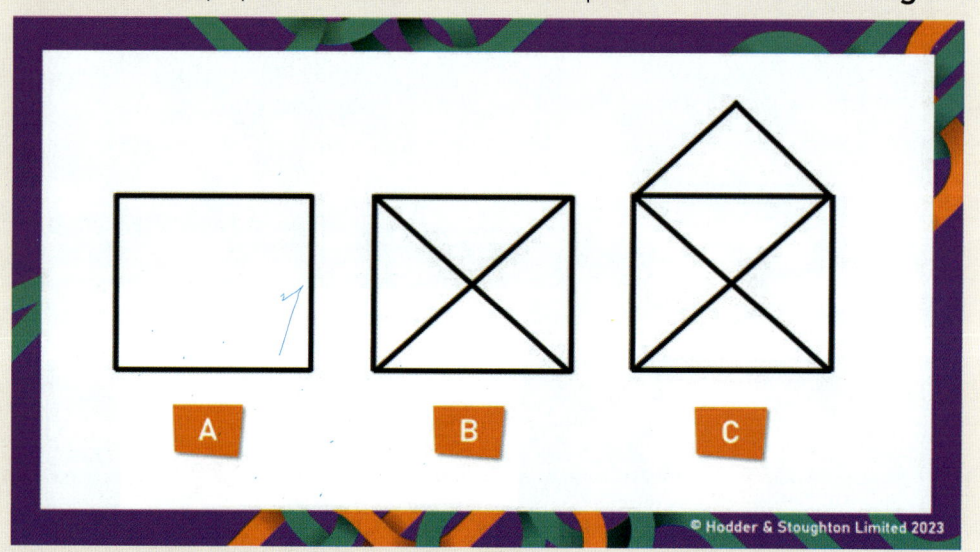

Taking each shape in turn, ask the pupils:

Can you draw all the lines of this shape just once without lifting your pencil off the paper?

3. Ask the pupils to rate each shape according to how challenging it was on a scale of 1 (easy) to 5 (very challenging). The pupils can indicate their opinions by a show of hands.

4 Develop the pupils' thinking further by looking at each shape in turn. Ask the pupils to reflect on:
What did you do to solve the problem?
Did you find it easy to solve?
Did you have to stick at it?

5 To encourage the pupils to reflect on their approach, share the reflection points:
Break it down.
Trial and error.
Need to do it a few times.
Which shapes did you manage to draw?
Which shapes are trickier?
What do you notice about the properties of each shape?

6 Share with the pupils the images of stickability (glue stick, sticky tack and sticky tape) on the **next teaching slide** and explain to them that:
Stickability is when we commit to a task and stick at it even if we find it challenging.

7 Ask the pupils to reflect on a time when they have shown stickability and to share their experience with a partner. Providing the pupils with time to reflect on the concept in their own experiences helps to reinforce it. Ask:
When have you shown stickability?

8 Select some of the pupils to share their experiences.

9 Share the solutions with the pupils using the **next teaching slide**:
a) and c) are possible.
b) is not possible.
It's possible if the number of odd vertices is either 0 or 2.
If there are zero odd vertices, you start and end at the same point.
If there are two odd vertices, these are your start and end points.
We call this an Euler circuit/path.

Follow up

Explore stickability in the context of the pupils' learning, e.g. when they find something new difficult.

Create a display to capture the pupils' experiences when they have shown stickability.

Pupils' responses

What did you do to solve the problem?

> 'Elaborate patterns.'
>
> 'Lots of attempts.'
>
> 'Failed'
>
> 'Cheated!'

When have you shown stickability?

> 'I showed stickability in the maths challenge, as the hard questions at the end needed a lot of thinking.'
>
> 'In dancing, I showed stickability as there was a hard step to learn.'
>
> 'When I was playing football, I kept trying to score a goal but failed to. I kept trying though.'

4 Stickability

A pupil's attempts at solving the problem

5 On track

Summary

This session encourages pupils to identify an area in which they wish to challenge themselves. It using visioning techniques to reinforce the steps to success and how we can break challenges down into achievable steps.

Focus

Developing control, challenge, commitment and confidence

Outcome

To identify an area in which they wish to challenge themselves
To identify how they can break down their challenges into smaller steps

Resources

Teaching slides: Year 5 Session 5
A large sheet of paper

Session

1. Arrange the pupils so they can see the board and then share with them the image of the track using the **teaching slide**.

2. Explain to the pupils that we can identify areas in which we want to improve ourselves and set ourselves a challenge. Reinforce the idea that everyone is different and will have their own individual challenge; that it is not a race against others but a way of visualising their individual steps to success; and that visualising can help us be successful and work effectively towards our goals.

3. Encourage the pupils to reflect on the area in which they want to challenge themselves. Provide the pupils with some thinking time to reflect on this.

4   Ask a few pupils to share their ideas. Ensure that their challenges are specific, e.g. improving my drawing skills rather than getting better at art.

5   Explain to the pupils that you want them to close their eyes and, using a soft, calm voice:

Visible Thinking

Explain that you want them to visualise a racetrack. At the end of the racetrack is the challenge that they want to achieve, e.g. learning to dive, improving in maths when solving mathematical word problems or improving your writing of non-chronological reports. Ask the pupils to think about how the challenge can be broken into smaller steps that they can achieve on the way – milestones where they can be successful. They should think about how they can break down their challenge into three or four smaller steps and think about the order in which they want to achieve these steps.

6   You may wish to model recording a challenge on a racetrack. Draw this on a piece of paper and, as you do, ask the pupils to support you in breaking down the challenge into smaller achievable steps.

Visible Thinking

I want to improve my writing of diaries and improve my sentences. I think I need to collect really powerful words. I am going to get a notebook and write them down. I should probably read more books to help me. I find it hard to use different connectives so I think another step could be practising using them. I am going to ask my teacher for feedback on how to improve and then I am going to write a diary regularly and include all of these steps.

7   Pupils should then record their challenge broken down into the different steps.

8   Ask the pupils to share their challenge with a partner and explain to each other how they are going to work towards achieving their challenges:
    How can I break this down into smaller steps?
    What would be achievable?
    Think about the things you can do to get better.
    Chunk it into the different steps like things you could practise and who could help you.
    Think about what you should do first.
    Talk it through with a friend.

SESSIONS FOR 9–10-YEAR-OLDS (YEAR 5)

> **Follow up**
>
> Ask the pupils to write instructions on how to be on track and break down a challenge into smaller steps.
>
> Pupils could work as mentors for younger children and help them identify a challenge and break it down into achievable steps. They could act as a mini-coach and meet with the children to encourage them on their journey.

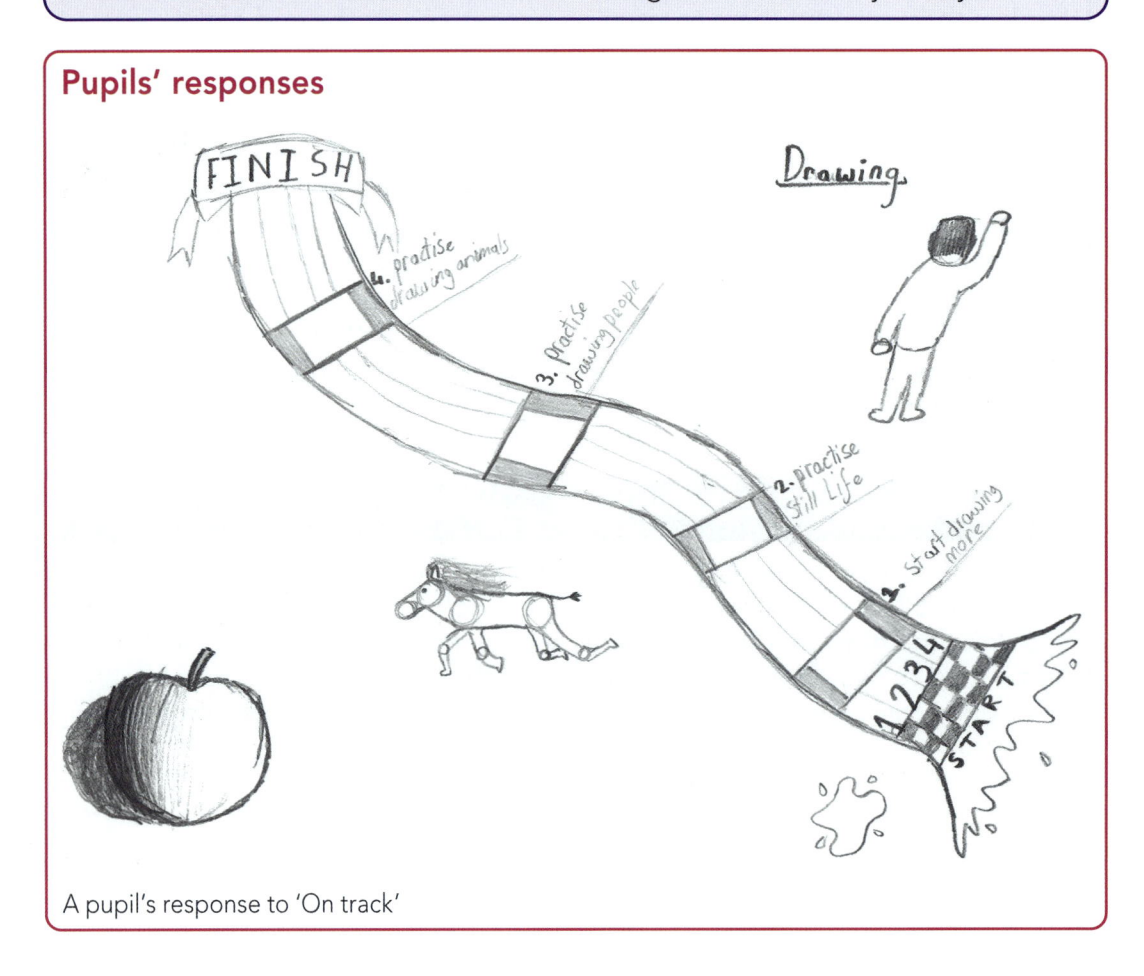

Pupils' responses

A pupil's response to 'On track'

6 Network audit

Summary

This session introduces the network audit, a simple tool that helps develop control and confidence. Pupils examine the people in their network and start to build a list of people that they can call upon in difficult times.

Focus

Developing control and confidence

Outcome

To create their own personal network audit

Resources

Teaching slides: Year 5 Session 6

Session

1. Arrange the pupils so they are sitting with a partner and can see the board clearly.
2. Explain to the pupils that:
   You all have a network of people around you who would be happy to help you.
   It is a myth that in order to be successful 'you must stand on your own two feet'. Often, we feel that asking for help is a sign of weakness or failure. This is, in fact, untrue as many successful people simply have the confidence to ask for help and advice to get to where they want to be.
3. Most pupils find that there are lots of people around them who can support them; some they use quite frequently, others less so. They build a visual network of support, making them more aware of the support they have.
   Ask the pupils to think about all the people they have around them who can give them advice or help with things they are struggling with.
4. You may wish to model your own examples to the pupils:

> **Visible Thinking**
>
> My dad helps me to fix things and my friend Kelly is very good at listening to me when I have a problem.

Sessions for 9–10-year-olds (Year 5)

5. Pose the question to the pupils:
   Who helps you?
   Provide the pupils with some thinking time and then select some individuals to share their experiences.

6. Share the structure of a network audit with the pupils using the **teaching slide**. Explain that they are at the centre and around them are all the people willing to support them. You may wish to have created your own personal audit and to share this with the pupils.

7. Explain that the different people who support us can be categorised in different ways, e.g:
   - people who help us in practical ways
   - people who help us improve.

8. Provide the pupils with some time to create their own network audit, writing in the names of some of the people in each of the categories who they could call upon for help and advice.

Follow up

Create a network audit for different scenarios at school or at home, for example:
Who can I talk to if I am worried about my friend at school?
If I want to get better at maths, who can help me and how?

Pupils' responses

6 NETWORK AUDIT

My network

Ben (My brother): Ben supports me with the homework that I'm stuck on that my parents can't do.

Dad: My dad helps around the house and cooking. He also helps me with my running and Netball training.

Mum: Supports me with all my music and work side of life.

Chloe: My best friend in the whole world. Supports me 24/7 with whatever I need.

Doctors: Doctors help with all my medical needs.

Family: Other family members support me with all my after school clubs and activities.

Teachers: Teachers support me with all of my academic needs. They are also there for anything I want help with.

Friends: Best friends support and understand anything you need them to.

Pupils' responses to 'My network audit'

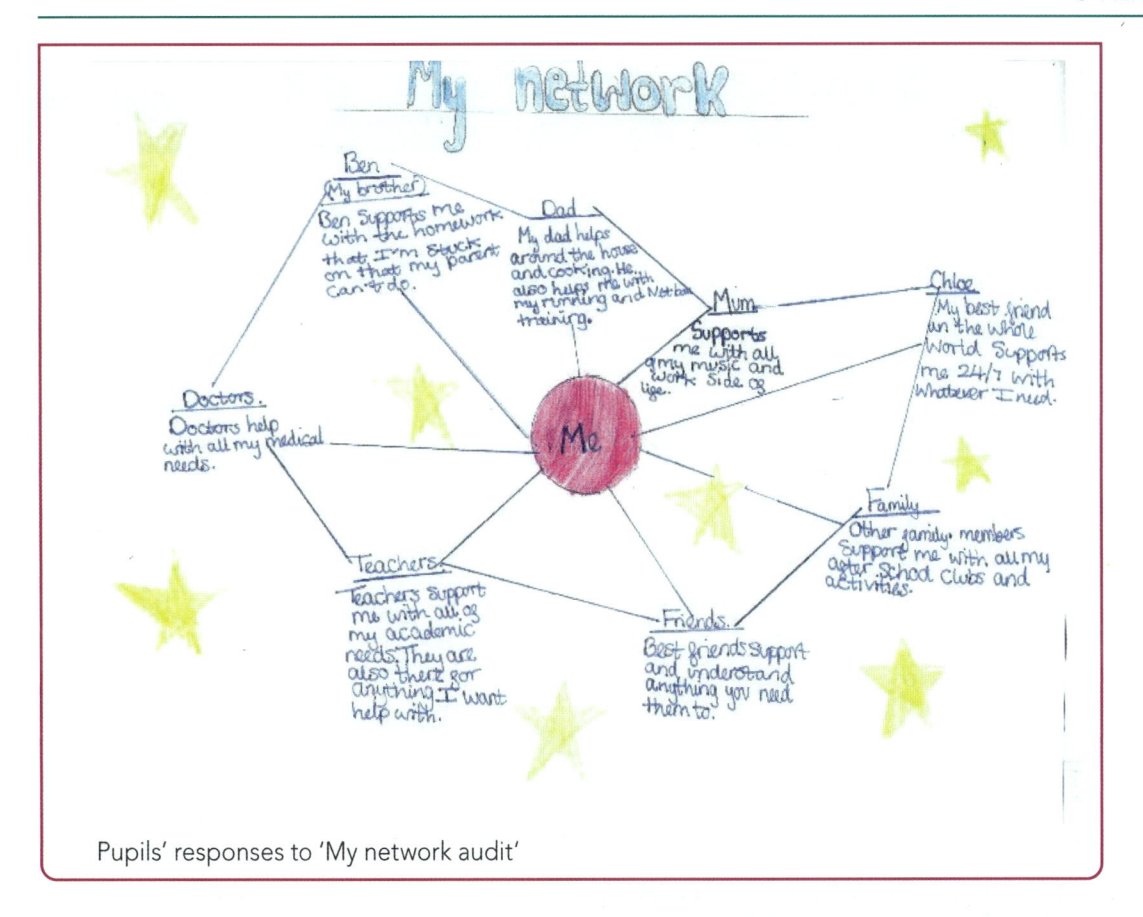

SESSIONS FOR 9–10-YEAR-OLDS (YEAR 5)

7 Just a minute

Summary

This session introduces pupils to the idea of procrastination and simple techniques to overcome it.

Focus

Developing control and commitment

Outcome

To identify ways of overcoming procrastination

Resources

Teaching slides: Year 5 Session 7
Timer (optional)

Session

1. Sit the pupils in a circle and place the timer in the centre of the circle. Display the **first teaching slide** and ask the pupils if they have ever been asked to do something by an adult and responded with 'Just a minute!'
2. Set a timer (either a physical one or using the **next teaching slide**) for a minute and ask the pupils to focus on how long it takes. Watch it together silently. This will help them to understand how long a minute is.
3. Explain to the pupils that we waste minutes all of the time by avoiding doing things and that these minutes add up.
4. Explain to the pupils that we all often procrastinate, which means that we delay doing something or put something off. We often procrastinate if we are nervous about doing something or are reluctant to do it, from tidying up our bedroom to completing our homework. We all frequently procrastinate, and it leads to us being less productive.

Visible Thinking

Share an example of when you have procrastinated.

5 Ask the pupils to reflect on:
Have you ever procrastinated?

6 Ask the pupils to share times when they have procrastinated. Develop their thinking further by probing them:
Why did you procrastinate?
How did you feel when you were procrastinating?

7 Explain to the pupils that there are different strategies that we can use to prevent ourselves from procrastinating.

8 Talk through the following strategies with the pupils, explaining clearly why you would choose to use each one and the process you go through.

Just a minute! – beginning the task promptly and seeing what you can produce in just a minute (or five).

Explain to the pupils that this strategy is particularly useful when we have to write, as it encourages us to get some ideas on paper as a first draft and prevents us from avoiding putting pen to paper. Remind the pupils that a first draft is your first attempt and that it can be redrafted and improved.

Model this strategy with a piece of writing.

Chunking – breaking the task down into achievable stages.

Explain to the pupils that at times a task can seem too big or too challenging so we avoid starting it. We can therefore chunk it into small, achievable steps.

Model this strategy using the context of homework, chunking it into smaller achievable steps on sticky notes.

Priorities – identifying the things that we need to do first.

Explain to the pupils that, to prevent ourselves from procrastinating, we need to identify our priorities. These can be classified into things that need to be done:
- urgently
- as soon as you can
- by a deadline
- when you have free time.

Explain to the pupils that they have four things they want to do:
- Play on their device.
- Practise their spellings.
- Write their diary.
- Phone their friend.

Ask the pupils to discuss with their partner which of these should be their priority.

Ask the pupils to share their thoughts and then develop this further by asking them to order the activities in terms of priorities.

SESSIONS FOR 9–10-YEAR-OLDS (YEAR 5)

5 Provide each group with one of the scenarios on the **handouts**. Initially, give them a few minutes to read and discuss their scenario. Ask the pupils to focus their discussions on:

How does … feel?

What are the main difficulties?

Dear Agony Aunt…

Doug is nervous as he has an upcoming football match is very important to his team. He has played well recently and everyone is expecting him to score but he is worried he will let them down. He is having problems sleeping.

What should he do?

© Hodder & Stoughton Limited 2023

Dear Agony Aunt…

Daanya is nervous about attending a residential as she has to stay overnight away from home. She has never done this and is scared that she will get upset and want to go home. She hasn't told anyone she is feeling like this. She is thinking that she might pretend to be ill so she doesn't have to go.

What should she do?

© Hodder & Stoughton Limited 2023

Agony Aunt scenarios

6 Then develop the discussions further by asking the pupils to consider how the 4Cs can support the pupils with their problems. You may wish to provide them with a grid to record their ideas on.

8 AGONY AUNT

> **7** Once the pupils' discussions are underway you can develop them further by sharing these prompts on the **next teaching slide**:
> *How could they show … (control, challenge, commitment, confidence)?*
> *What can they do?*
> *What could others say?*
> *What could they say to themselves?*
>
> **8** Provide the pupils with some time to discuss their responses.
>
> **9** Once the discussions have drawn to a conclusion, select a scenario (also on the **next two teaching slides**) and ask the groups to respond. Focus their responses on:
> *How can … take control of their problem?*
> *Will challenge help …?*
> *How can commitment support …?*
> *How can confidence be used to support … with their problem?*
>
> **10** Repeat for the other scenario and take feedback from the pupils:
> *Did the 4Cs help you to respond to the problems?*

Follow up

Pupils could create their own scenarios that other pupils can reflect on.
Create visual prompts to display in the classroom to support the pupils when they have problems.

Pupils' responses

How does … feel? What are the main difficulties?
Doug
> 'He can't sleep.'
> 'He is nervous.'
> 'He is lacking confidence.'

Daanya
> 'She is nervous about something that is going to happen.'
> 'Worried about not seeing her parents.'
> 'She is thinking of faking being ill.'

Sessions for 9–10-year-olds (Year 5)

How can ... take control of their problem? Will challenge help ...? How can commitment support ...? How can confidence be used to support ... with their problem?

Commitment
Be committed to your football team, then they won't care if you fail. They'll get over it.

Control
Control your anxiety, and relax and believe in yourself. Maybe tell an adult about your sleeping problems.

Challenge
Challenge yourself to do your best. It does not matter if you fail.

Confidence
Try to be more confident in your own abilitys. You can do it!!!!!
Try and have fun. Practice.
Believe in yourself!
It's not the end of the world!!!

A pupil's response to Doug's problem

Control
practise going beforehand with a sleepover maybe.
Take something that will remind you of home.

Commitment
try make her self go

Challenge
to actually go

Confidence
"Tell an adult that she is nervous in the situation.
Think about the positives.
It could be fun

A pupil's response to Daanya's problem

Did the 4Cs help you to respond to the problems?

'Using the 4Cs gave it a context.'

'Helped me to think in different ways.'

'Helped me to think of different words.'

Sessions for 10–11-year-olds (Year 6)

Title	Focus	Outcomes	Summary	Page
1 I am unique	Developing confidence	To identify what makes us unique To identify our strengths	This session asks pupils to reflect on their strengths and what makes them unique. They create a jigsaw puzzle of themselves made up of their strengths and unique qualities.	197
2 Myth of intelligence	Developing control, challenge, commitment and confidence	To reflect on their perceptions of intelligence To explore evidence that challenges the belief that we are born with set intelligence	This session shares research about the brain and develops pupils' understanding of the concept of intelligence.	200
3 Circles of control	Developing, control, challenge, commitment and confidence	To identify aspects of their lives that can be controlled To reflect on how the circles of control can be used to support them to deal with problems	This session explores Stephen Covey's model of the 'circles of control' and encourages pupils to reflect on what they can control and how they can be proactive.	204

Title	Focus	Outcomes	Summary	Page
4 Going with the flow	Developing control, challenge, commitment and confidence	To reflect on how they can be in a focused state	This session introduces the idea of getting into a focused state, explores what this looks like and asks pupils to consider how they behave in this state.	208
5 Passion project	Developing control, challenge, commitment and confidence	To identify what helps us to be committed to a task	This session asks pupils to reflect on something that they have stuck at over a period of time. Pupils identify factors that have contributed to this and their success.	213
6 Change	Developing control, challenge, commitment and confidence	To reflect on how we respond to change	This session explores how we approach change, including transition to secondary school.	217
7 SMART goals	Developing control, challenge, commitment and confidence	To identify a goal. To break down a goal into a SMART goal	This session introduces the model of SMART goals, and encourages pupils to use this structure to reflect on something they wish to improve at.	221
8 Inner critic	Developing control, challenge, commitment and confidence	To explore strategies to help pupils deal with their negative critic. To challenge their critic and change negative messages into positive messages	This session encourages pupils to reflect on their own inner critic and its impact, and to explore how an alternative voice can support them.	225

Overview

The focus for the Year 6 sessions is to review all of the different aspects of mental toughness and to provide pupils with the tools and practical strategies to support them both in Year 6 and as they transition into secondary school.

1 I am unique

Summary

This session asks pupils to reflect on their strengths and what makes them unique. They create a jigsaw puzzle of themselves made up of their strengths and unique qualities.

Focus

Developing confidence

Outcome

To identify what makes us unique
To identify our strengths

Resources

Teaching slides: Year 6 Session 1
Handout: Jigsaw person template
Visualiser

Session

1. Arrange the pupils so they are sitting where they can see the board clearly.
2. Explain to them that you are going to be reflecting on what makes us unique and special. Recognising what makes us unique and what contributes to this helps to develop our confidence.

3. Share with the pupils the image of the jigsaw person on the **teaching slide**.

4. Explain to the pupils that we are all unique and that we are made up of our different experiences, behaviours, qualities, hobbies, things we care about and the important people in our lives. Although we are all different, everyone is made up of their strengths, experiences and abilities.

5. Using the jigsaw person template, model what makes you unique, your strengths, interests and significant people in your life. You may wish to do this under a visualiser so the pupils can see what you are doing while you explain. Ensure that you model clearly why you have included each aspect and why it is important to you.

Visible Thinking

I am including writing as I enjoy doing it and I have worked hard to improve at it as I am dyslexic. My daughter is important to me as I love her more than anything. Tennis is important as I enjoy playing it.

6. Once you have shared a few examples, provide the pupils with the jigsaw person template **handout** and explain that you want them to create their own jigsaw person, including everything that is unique and important to them. Explain that they can record this however they like, including colour and drawings to represent the different aspects.

7. Provide the pupils with some time to complete their own jigsaw person.

8. Once they have completed them, randomly select a few pupils to share their jigsaw person. It would be useful to use a visualiser if you have one so that the whole class can see the image clearly.

9. Encourage each pupil who shares their jigsaw person to explain:
Why is each aspect important?

1 I AM UNIQUE

> **Follow up**
>
> Display the pupils' jigsaws in the classroom and refer to them regularly highlighting different strengths.
>
> Ask the pupils to choose someone they admire and create a person jigsaw.

Pupils' responses

Pupils' jigsaw people

Sessions for 10–11-year-olds (Year 6)

2 Myth of intelligence

Summary

This session shares research about the brain and develops pupils' understanding of the concept of intelligence.

Focus

Developing control, challenge, commitment and confidence

Outcome

To reflect on their perceptions of intelligence

To explore evidence that challenges the belief that we are born with set intelligence

Resources

Teaching slides: Year 6 Session 2
Handout: Facts about intelligence

Session

1. Arrange the pupils so they are sitting at a table with their partner and can see the board clearly.

2. The purpose of this session is to explore a key barrier to pupils achieving and one that can cause them to worry: the concept of being intelligent or clever. In the session, pupils are encouraged to reflect on their perceptions of intelligence. They are provided with evidence to dispel the myth that people are born intelligent and that this is fixed.

   Provide each pupil with the **handout**. Ask them to cut these up and then to work together to sort them into things they agree with, disagree with or are not sure about. Remind the pupils that you are interested in their opinions and that there are no right or wrong answers.

2 MYTH OF INTELLIGENCE

> ✂ You are born intelligent.
>
> You can grow and change your intelligence.
>
> Other people are always going to be more intelligent than me.
>
> I will never be good/clever at maths.
>
> The brain is like a muscle and can grow over time and new connections can be made.
>
> I can change my ability in a subject by working hard, asking teachers for help.
>
> Some people will never be intelligent.
>
> You can learn to do anything.

3 Reiterate that there are no right or wrong answers and that you are just interested in their opinions. Provide the pupils with some time to sort the statements and then take feedback. Ensure that you respond to the pupils' sorting and challenge any misconceptions. Ask them:

Which was the hardest statement to sort?
Why?
Why did you put … there?
Why do you believe this?

4 Explain to the pupils that our views of intelligence can often cause us to worry and to feel anxious about our own ability. In this session, you are going to address the myths of intelligence.

5 Share with the pupils the **first teaching slide** that dispels the myth of intelligence and ask the pupils to review their sorting of the statements in response to it.

The myth of intelligence

- Our brains are malleable and can develop and change over time due to experiences (learning) and other factors.
- As we learn we create new neurological pathways.
- Our intelligence is not fixed!
- We can get better at things even those we find tricky.

© Hodder & Stoughton Limited 2023

201

Sessions for 10–11-year-olds (Year 6)

6 Provide the pupils with some time and then ask them:
   Have you any comments/feedback on what has been shared with you?
   Did reflecting on this information change your sorting of the statements?

7 Take feedback from the pupils.

8 Develop their thinking further by sharing a definition of intelligence:
   Intelligence is the ability to acquire and apply knowledge and skills.

9 Share with the pupils the information about brain neuroplasticity on the **next teaching slide** and how this has developed over time. Again, ask the pupils to think about what they have read and then ask them:
   Have you any comments/feedback on what has been shared with you?

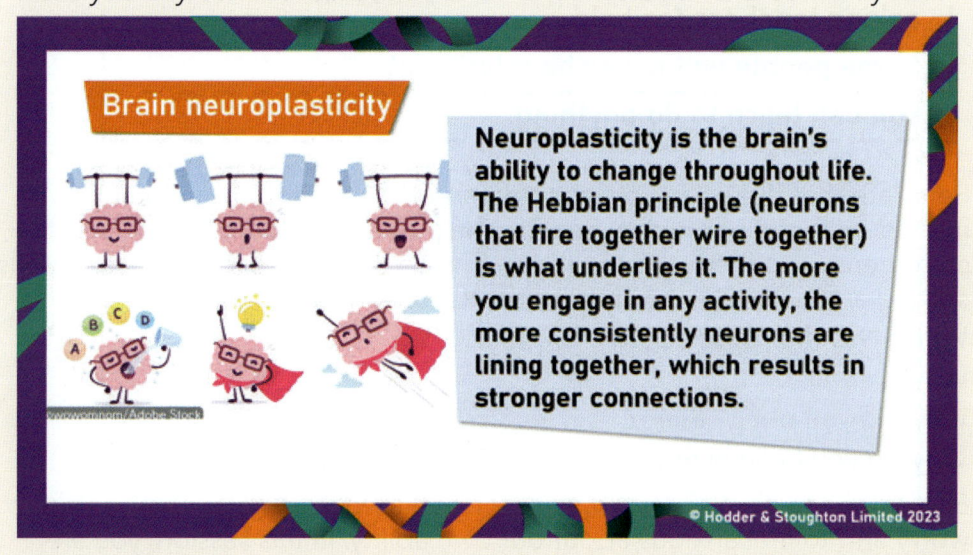

Brain neuroplasticity

Neuroplasticity is the brain's ability to change throughout life. The Hebbian principle (neurons that fire together wire together) is what underlies it. The more you engage in any activity, the more consistently neurons are lining together, which results in stronger connections.

© Hodder & Stoughton Limited 2023

10 Take feedback from the pupils and then ask them to revisit their original sorting of the statements. Ask them to consider:
   Do you wish to change any of your original ideas?

11 Give the pupils time to reflect and then ask them:
   Did you make any changes?
   If so, why?

Visible Thinking

Malleable means easily changed, for example changed into a different shape. Your brain is malleable as it can be changed as you learn new things. **Neurological pathways** are the connections in our brains formed by atoms to create synapses in the brain.

> **Follow up**
>
> Share with the pupils other examples of how the brain can develop, e.g. a taxi driver learning the knowledge or a young child learning to walk or talk.
>
> Revisit the statements regularly over time and ask the pupils to reflect on whether they would change how they have sorted them.

> **Pupils' responses**
>
> Which was the hardest statement to sort?
> - 'You are born intelligent – as some people can be good at things, like having an eye for art or an ear for music.'
> - 'I will never be good/clever at maths – you don't know about the future and there are different ways this can be interpreted.'
> - 'The brain is like a muscle – I was unsure of this one as I don't know if it is.'

SESSIONS FOR 10–11-YEAR-OLDS (YEAR 6)

3 Circles of control

Summary

This session explores Stephen Covey's model of the 'circles of control' and encourages pupils to reflect on what they can control and how they can be proactive.

Focus

Developing control, challenge, commitment and confidence

Outcome

To identify aspects of their lives that can be controlled
To reflect on how the circles of control can be used to support them to deal with problems

Resources

Teaching slides: Year 6 Session 3
Handout: Circles of control
Sticky notes

Session

1. Arrange the pupils so they are sitting with a partner and can see the board clearly.
2. Introduce Stephen Covey's 'circles of control' to the pupils using the **first teaching slide**:

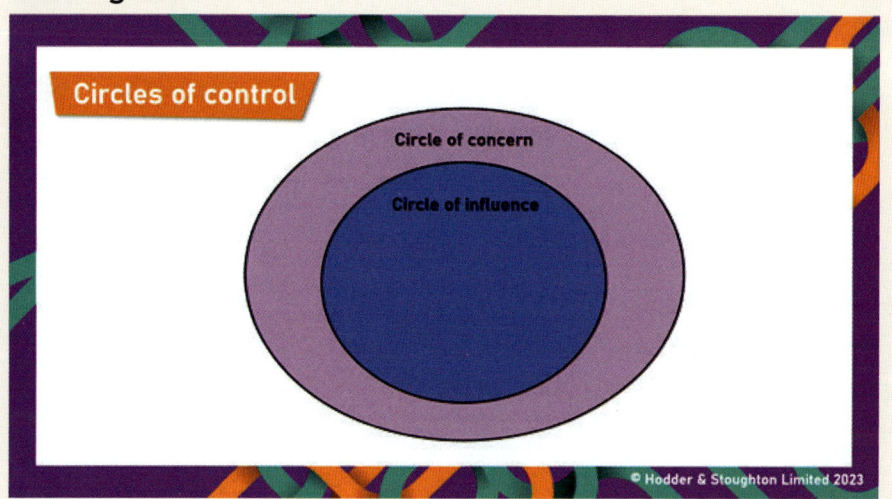

3. Explain to the pupils that Stephen Covey created this model so that we can put our worries into categories (or groups). He believed that the world around us is made of only two factors: the things we can control and the things we can't control. His explanation uses two circles: the circle of concern and the circle of influence.

4. Explain to the pupils that the circle of concern covers everything in our life that affects us. The circle of influence, on the other hand, includes everything within our life that we can have an effect on.

5. Explain that we can influence a lot of different aspects of our lives but not everything, e.g. you can't influence the weather, but you can control whether you eat the cake or not!

6. Explain to the pupils the difference between what we can control and what we can influence. To control means that we have complete authority over something, e.g. we can control whether we eat the cake or not. But we can't control whether our friend eats the cake. You might be able to convince your friend not to eat it. Or they might be inspired by you if you resist eating the cake. We can influence our friends, but we can't control them. Control means we can get exactly what we want; influence means we can have an impact, but cannot guarantee we will get the results we want.

7. Share with the pupils the updated model on the **next teaching slide**. Explain to the pupils that it helps to use a model such as this to review our challenges:

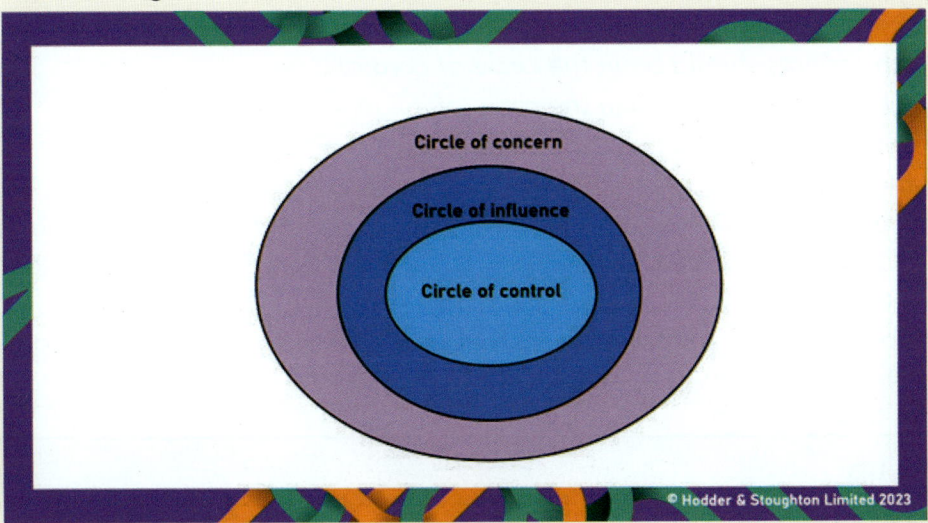

Circles of control 2

8. Ask the pupils to think about where the following statements would go on the second diagram:
   Eating healthy or unhealthy food.
   The train being late.
   Whether your friend agrees with your opinion.

SESSIONS FOR 10–11-YEAR-OLDS (YEAR 6)

9 Taking each statement in turn, ask the pupils to discuss their thoughts with a partner and then select pupils to share their thoughts.
Where would you place the statement?
Why would you put it there?

10 Develop the pupils' thinking further by showing them the case study about Su-Ling's day on the **next teaching slide**.

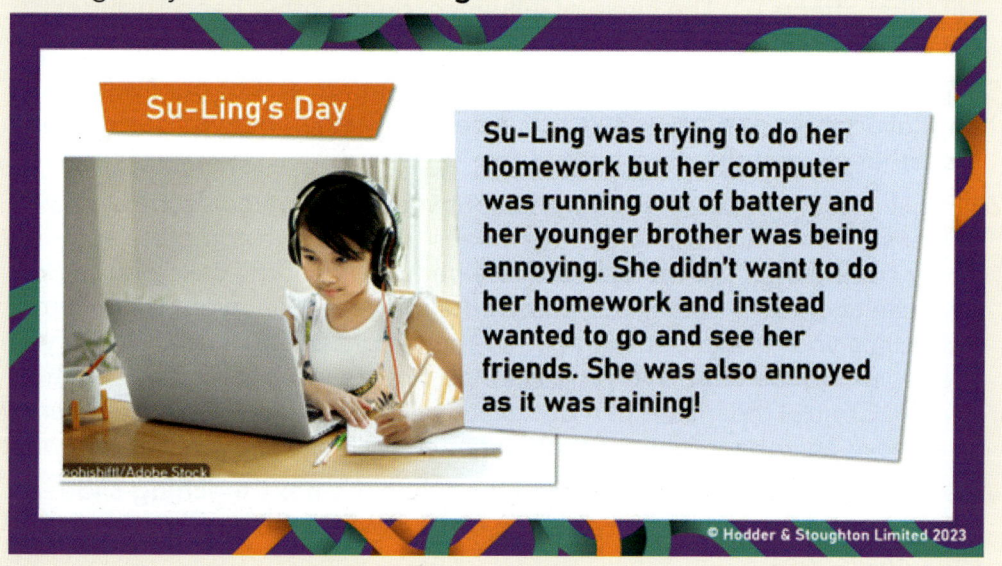

Su-Ling's Day

Su-Ling was trying to do her homework but her computer was running out of battery and her younger brother was being annoying. She didn't want to do her homework and instead wanted to go and see her friends. She was also annoyed as it was raining!

11 Ask the pupils to review Su-Ling's day and identify:
Which aspects should be in the circle of control?
Which aspects should be in the circle of influence?
Which aspects should be in the circle of concern?

12 Provide the pupils with the **handout** and some sticky notes. Ask them to work with a partner to identify the various aspects of Su-Ling's day and to write these onto the sticky notes.

13 Once the pupils have put their notes into their chosen circles, take feedback. If there are any aspects that they have not identified, highlight these and ask them to reflect on where they should be placed.

Follow up

The scenario could be personalised to contain issues that are of concern to your class.

Pupils could create their own circles to reflect their own challenges and problems.

3 Circles of Control

Pupils' responses

Which aspects should be in the circle of control?

Which aspects should be in the circle of influence?

Which aspects should be in the circle of concern?

Circles of Control

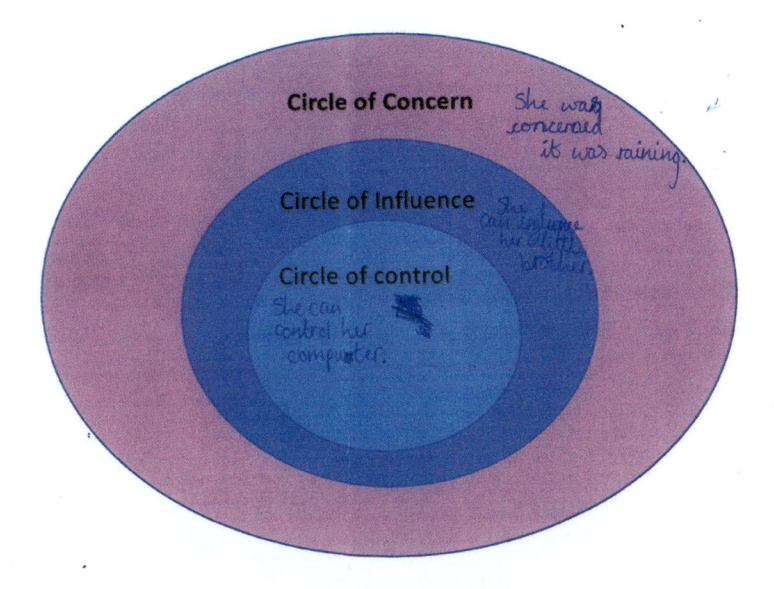

Circle of Concern — She was concerned it was raining.

Circle of Influence — She can influence her little brother.

Circle of control — She can control her computer.

A pupil's response to Su-Ling's day

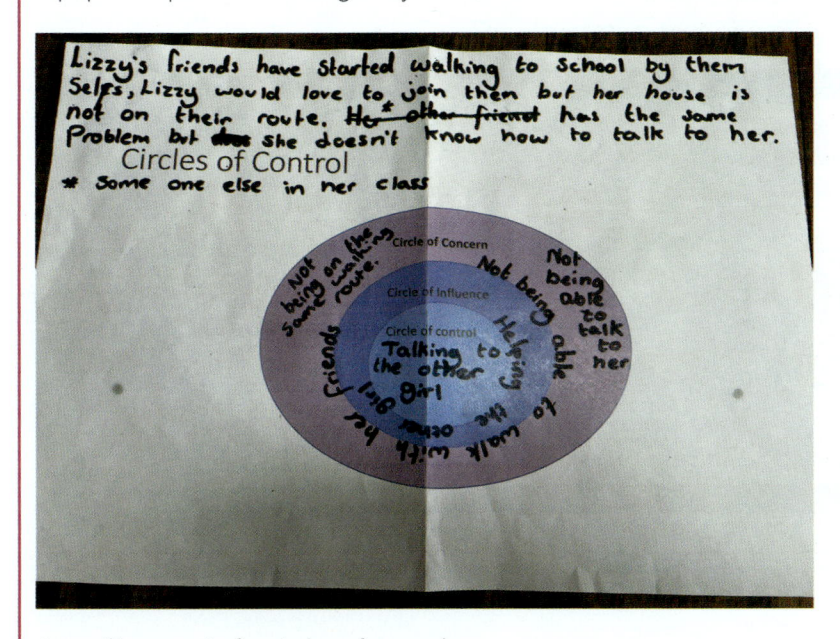

Lizzy's friends have started walking to school by themselves. Lizzy would love to join them but her house is not on their route. Her* other friend has the same problem but she doesn't know how to talk to her.

Circles of Control
* Some one else in her class

Circle of Concern — Not being on the same route. Not being able to talk to her.

Circle of Influence — Helping to walk with her friends. Ask the other girl.

Circle of control — Talking to the other girl.

A pupil's scenario for circles of control

207

SESSIONS FOR 10–11-YEAR-OLDS (YEAR 6)

4 Going with the flow

Summary

This session introduces the idea of getting into a focused state, explores what this looks like and asks pupils to consider how they behave in this state.

Focus

Developing control, challenge, commitment and confidence

Outcomes

To reflect on how they can be in a focused state

Resources

Teaching slides: Year 6 Session 4
Handout: Strategies to stay focused

Session

1. Arrange the pupils so they are sitting with a partner and can clearly see the board.
2. Share with the pupils the image of 'Be in a focused state' on the **first teaching slide** and ask them:
   What does being in a focused state mean?

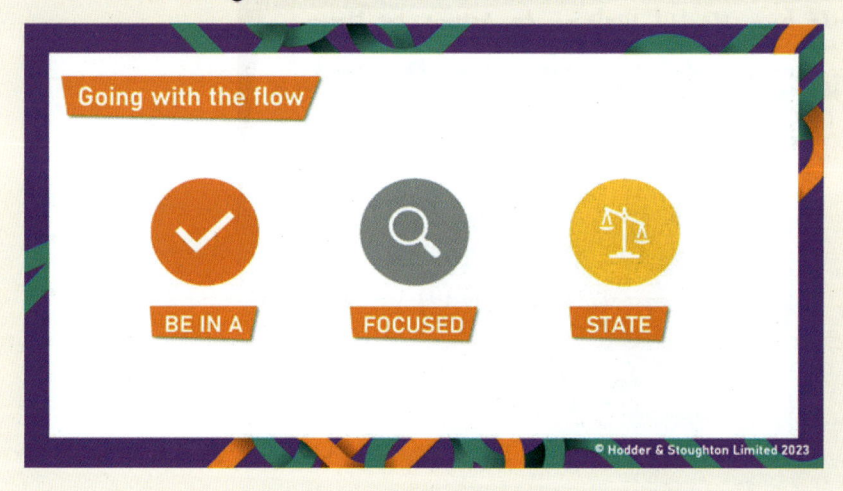

4 Going with the flow

3 Provide the pupils with some talk time and then take feedback from them. Encourage the pupils to expand their explanations and develop their thinking by asking them:
Tell me something more about that …

4 Share with the pupils the image of someone trying to work and being distracted on the **next teaching slide**.

Ask the pupils to discuss with their talk partner:
What does the word 'distraction' mean?

Visible Thinking

Distraction is a thing that prevents someone from concentrating on something, for example my friend talking when I try to listen in maths is a distraction.

5 Provide the pupils with some talk time and then ask them to share their ideas.

6 Develop the pupils' thinking further by asking them to reflect on:
What distracts you?

7 You may wish to model what distracts you and why:

Visible Thinking

I get distracted by my phone and I find myself looking at lots of different things on it rather than focusing on my work.

8 Again, take feedback from the pupils and create a list of the key distractions.

209

9 Explain to the pupils that they can take control of their distractions and be in a focused state.

10 Explain to the pupils that being in a focused state means: sticking with the task at hand – the work you have to do, continuing to work towards whatever you need to do and ensuring that you stay concentrated on one activity.

11 On the **next teaching slide**, share with the pupils the slide containing the different strategies they can use to stay in a focused state:

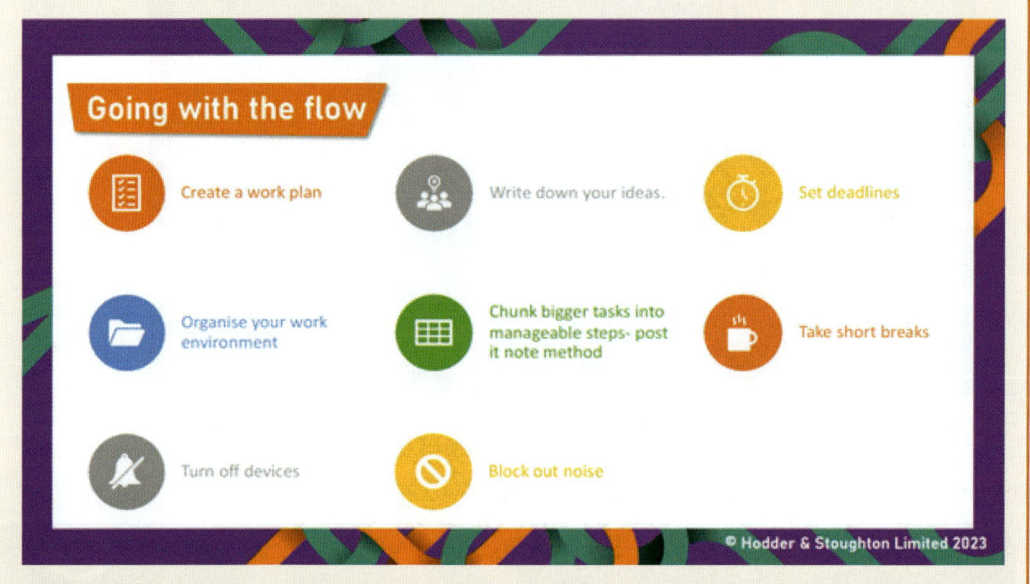

Going with the flow

- Create a work plan
- Write down your ideas.
- Set deadlines
- Organise your work environment
- Chunk bigger tasks into manageable steps- post it note method
- Take short breaks
- Turn off devices
- Block out noise

© Hodder & Stoughton Limited 2023

12 Ensure the pupils are listening as you explain each strategy in turn and provide examples:

Create a work plan – make a list of what you need to do and then use this to create a plan of when you are going to do it.

Write down your ideas – have a notepad where you can jot down your ideas so you don't lose them. You never know when you might think of something amazing!

Set deadlines – make sure you set clear deadlines for a task and avoid doing things at the last minute. Try to set a deadline that is some time before something is due, so you have time to check it, e.g. if your homework is due on Friday then set a deadline of Wednesday so you have time to check it.

Organise your work environment – make sure you have a quiet place to work that is clear, so you are not distracted. Take some time to clear your desk and get the equipment you might need ready. You will find that you are more productive.

Chunk bigger tasks into manageable steps – breaking down a big piece of work into smaller chunks helps us to be more successful. (You may wish to model this strategy by using sticky notes and chunking a task the pupils have been given.)

Take short breaks – taking short breaks for 5–10 minutes when you are practising/learning helps you to be more effective. For example, you could focus for 30 minutes and then take a short break.

Turn off devices – this is the hardest thing to do. We can all get lost in our phones and devices for hours, but they have a negative effect on our ability to focus. So, put them somewhere safe and set a time when you can look at them again.

Block out noise – we are all different, but it is easy to get distracted by noise, whether it's your friend chatting to you in class or loud music being played. But you can take control. You can ask your friend to stop talking and you can choose to work somewhere quiet. It's up to you.

13 Explain to the pupils that you want them to think about the different strategies. You may wish to provide them with the **handout** that summarises the ideas. Ask them to think about:
Which strategy will you try? Why?

14 Provide the pupils with some time to reflect and then ask them to share which strategies they intend to try.

Follow up

Model using the different strategies in different lessons, e.g. chunking a piece of writing into sections or breaking down a task involving research into smaller activities.

Revisit the strategies the pupils decided to try and take feedback on how successful they were and what they might do differently.

Pupils' responses

What does being in a focused state mean?

'Being very focused on something. You put your whole mind on it.'

'Focusing on one thing.'

'Not letting people distract you.'

What does the word 'distraction' mean?

'Taking you away from what you need to do.'

'Something getting in your way of doing something.'

What distracts you?

'If I am doing my homework, I will go to put music on and put the TV on instead!'

'My dad does! I want to play my game and my dad makes me wash the pots!'

'When I am doing my homework, I think about the things I would rather be doing!'

'The Year 6 WhatsApp group!'

'My phone.'

'Devices.'

Which strategy will you try? Why?

'I will try chunking into smaller tasks – I think it's a better approach.'

'Creating a tidy work environment so I don't get distracted.'

'Turning off my devices – although that will be hard.'

'Set deadlines so I am not doing things last minute.'

5 Passion project

Summary

This session asks pupils to reflect on something that they have stuck at over a period of time. Pupils identify factors that have contributed to this and their success.

Focus

Developing control, challenge, commitment and confidence

Outcomes

To identify what helps us to be committed to a task

Resources

Teaching slides: Year 6 Session 5

Session

1. Arrange the pupils so they are sitting with a partner and can clearly see the board.
2. Introduce the idea of being passionate about something. Share with them something you are passionate about, e.g. a hobby or a sport. Explain to the pupils why you are passionate about it and how hard you have had to work to improve at it.
3. Ask the pupils to reflect on:
   What are you passionate about?
   Why?
4. Provide the pupils with some thinking time and then ask them to share some examples.
5. Introduce Ned's passion project on the **first teaching slide** and share the key information about his passion for art.

> **Passion Project**
> - Ned wants to improve his artwork and create a piece of art in the style of Picasso.
> - He has been watching YouTube clips to learn new techniques.
> - He is spending an hour every day practising.

6 Ask the pupils to think about Ned and discuss with a partner:
How is Ned showing stickability?
If the pupils are unfamiliar with the term 'stickability', ask other pupils to remind them with a definition.

7 Provide the pupils with some talk time and then take feedback from them.

8 During the feedback, ensure that the key factors are highlighted, including time, learning and role models.

9 Develop the pupils' thinking further and introduce them to Dior's passion project on the **next teaching slide**. Share the key information about his passion for football.

> **Passion Project**
> - Dior loves football and really wants to get into the school team.
> - He wasn't selected the last time he tried.
> - He has joined a football club and been having lessons.
> - He practices in the garden with his older brother every night.

10 Ask the pupils to think about Dior and discuss with a partner:
How is Dior showing stickability?

11 Provide the pupils with some talk time and then take feedback from them.

12 Again, reinforce the key characteristics of stickability, including trying again, and overcoming barriers and emotions.

13 Develop the pupils' thinking further by asking them:
What else could Dior do to show stickability?

14 Provide the pupils with some talk time and then take feedback from them.

Follow up

Ask the pupils to think about their passion project and how they could show greater stickability.

Ask the pupils to create their own case studies featuring their passion project and explain how they have shown stickability.

The passion project case studies can be adapted to represent the interests of pupils in your class and ways they can behave to show stickability.

Pupils' responses

What are you passionate about?
- '*Swimming.*'
- '*Horse riding.*'
- '*Drawing.*'
- '*Dancing.*'
- '*Playing football.*'

How is Ned showing stickability?
- '*Spending an hour every day.*'
- '*Learning new techniques.*'
- '*Looking at the work of artists who are good.*'
- '*He wants to improve.*'

How is Dior showing stickability?
- '*He is sad but he tries again. But if you don't feel sad and show emotions then you're not human.*'
- '*Trying again.*'
- '*Joining another football club for extra practice.*'
- '*Practising with his friends.*'

What else could Dior do to show stickability?

'Watch clips of footballers learning new skills.'

'Find someone who is a good footballer and ask for help.'

'Join another football club for even more practice.'

My passion project

'I am passionate about swimming because I like it and I show commitment to it by the progress I have made. I like to compete, so I have to train hard. I find that being in the water makes me feel less stressed and I like that. I have also met lots of friends there.'

'I showed commitment because at the start I kept sinking but I wanted to get better at it. I wanted to get better as I liked doing it. I showed commitment because I was the worst in my group, but I wanted to get better and compete against others.'

6 Change

Summary

This session explores how we approach change, including transition to secondary school.

Focus

Developing control, challenge, commitment and confidence

Outcomes

To reflect on how we respond to change

Resources

Teaching slides: Year 6 Session 6
Handout: Changes
Handout: Changes relating to secondary school transition

Session

1. Arrange the pupils so they are sitting with a partner and can see the board.
2. Reveal the word 'change' on the **teaching slide** and ask the pupils to think about:
   What does the word 'change' mean?
3. Provide the pupils with some talk time and then take feedback from them.
4. Explain to the pupils that change is inevitable (it will happen). There can be small and big changes and we can't control them. People change, things change, and we change.
5. Develop the pupils' thinking further by asking the pupils to think about:
   What has changed in your life?
6. Provide the pupils with some talk time and then take feedback from them. While the pupils are sharing their personal changes, probe their thinking further by asking them:
   How did you feel about the change?

7. Share with the pupils the **handout** with different changes on. Ask them to cut this up and then to work with a partner to sort the pieces into significant and minor changes. You may wish to adapt the changes to reflect issues in your classroom or you may wish to select the **handout** which relates to transition to secondary school.

✂ -
- Moving to a new house.
- Having a new baby brother/sister.
- Your teacher being absent, so you have a supply teacher.
- Having to move seats in class.
- Changing schools.
- Falling out with your friend.
- Your friend changing your plans as they have to go somewhere with their family.
- Your football lesson being cancelled.

Changes

✂ -
- Not seeing my friends.
- Getting a detention.
- People being unkind to me.
- Not knowing my teachers.
- Having a lot more homework.
- Getting lost in a new school.
- Scared of being around so many people.
- Having to make friends.

Changes relating to secondary school transition

8. Provide the pupils with some time to sort the statements into significant and minor changes. Remind them that there are no right or wrong answers and that you are just interested in their opinions.

9. Take feedback from the pupils and recreate their sorting on the board so it is easy for everyone to see.

10. Select one of the changes that the pupils are worried about and ask them to discuss with their talk partner:

    What can you do to help reduce how you feel about the change?

11. You may wish to model how you would respond to one of the changes. For example, for the concern about getting lost, you could reduce your worries by getting a map of school and looking at it the night before.

12. Provide the pupils with some time to discuss their ideas with their partner and then take feedback from them.

> **Follow up**
>
> The activity could be adapted to explore change in different contexts and be made relevant to the pupils' own experiences.
>
> Pupils can illustrate how they would respond and use the 4Cs to approach the change.

Pupils' responses

What does the word 'change' mean?

'Something being different.'

'You can change your perspective.'

'Going from one thing to another thing which isn't the same.'

'Change – not the same as it used to be.'

'Change your personality.'

'In sport, you can change your strategy.'

What has changed in your life?

'My height – that's a physical change.'

'Getting older.'

'We get a new teacher every year.'

'Moving to a new house.'

'Getting a pet.'

'My cat went missing.'

How did you feel about the change?

'Moving to a new house made me feel happy as I got a new bedroom.'

'I felt sad when my cat went missing.'

'I was overwhelmed when I had to move to a new house.'

SESSIONS FOR 10–11-YEAR-OLDS (YEAR 6)

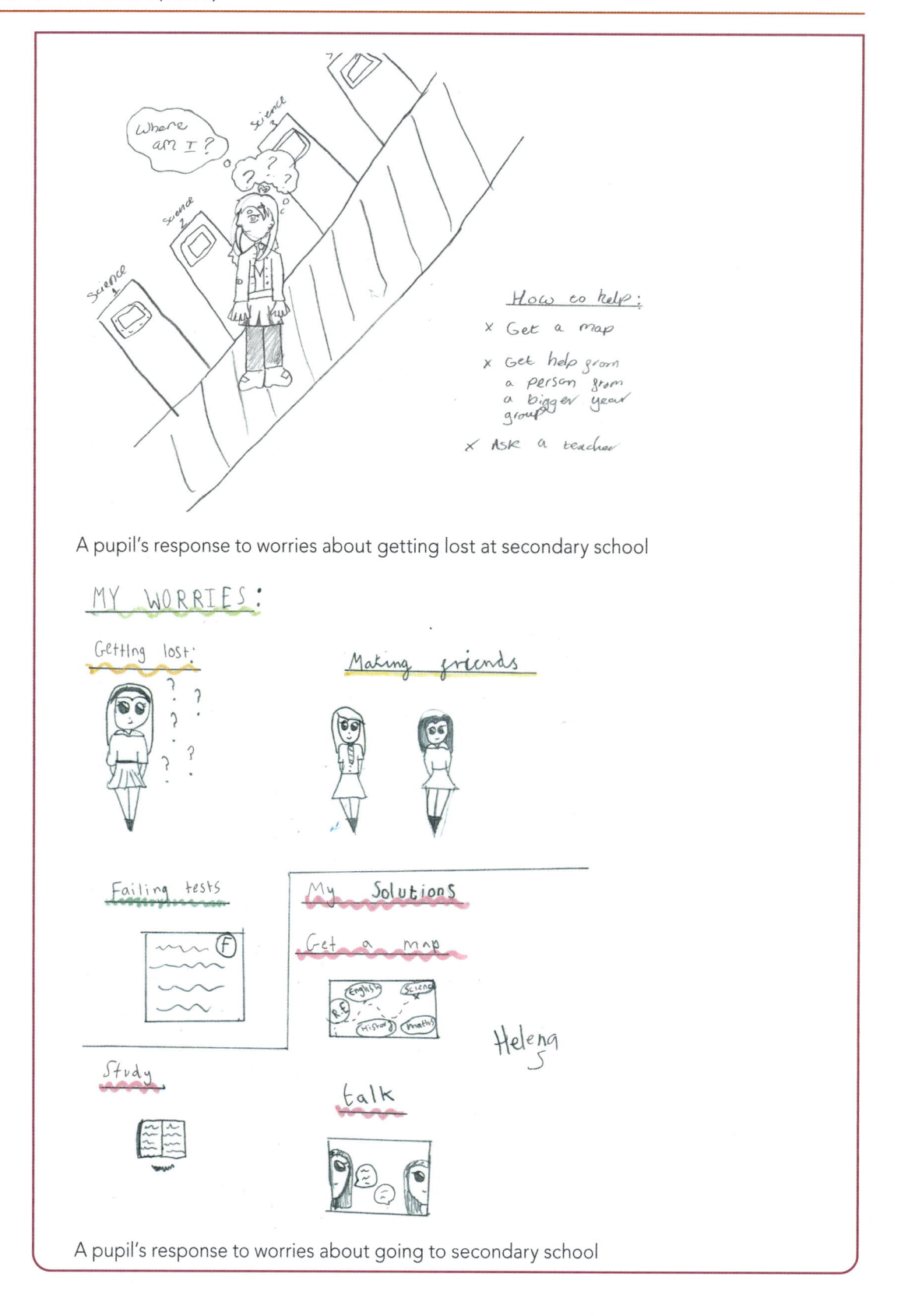

A pupil's response to worries about getting lost at secondary school

A pupil's response to worries about going to secondary school

7 SMART goals

Summary

This session introduces the model of SMART goals, and encourages pupils to use this structure to reflect on something they wish to improve at.

Focus

Developing control, challenge, commitment and confidence

Outcome

To identify a goal
To break down a goal into a SMART goal

Resources

Teaching slides: Year 6 Session 7
Handout: SMART goals
Visualiser

Session

1. Arrange the pupils so they are sitting with a partner and able to see the board clearly.
2. Explain to the pupils that they are going to be reflecting on setting goals. Ask the pupils to discuss:
   What does the word 'goal' mean?
3. Give the pupils time to discuss their ideas and then take feedback. You may need to clarify that by goals you are thinking in the context of setting goals not scoring a goal on a football pitch.
4. During the feedback, encourage the pupils to listen to each other's ideas and build upon them:
   Can you bounce/build on from …'s idea?

> **Visible Thinking**
>
> A **goal** is a target that you have identified – something you want to learn how to do or get better at. It is something that you are aiming for.

5. Explain to the pupils that, when setting goals, it important that we make them SMART.

6. Using the **teaching slide**, explain to the pupils that goals can be changed into SMART goals. Explain that this means:

   Specific – be precise as you can, not general.

   Measurable – How will you know when you have reached your goal?

   Action-based – What can you do to get the goal started? How? What's step 1? What's step 2?

   Realistic – Has someone done it before? Could you speak to that person? What previous personal successes are connected to the goal?

   Time-bound – When do you want to do this by? Be precise!

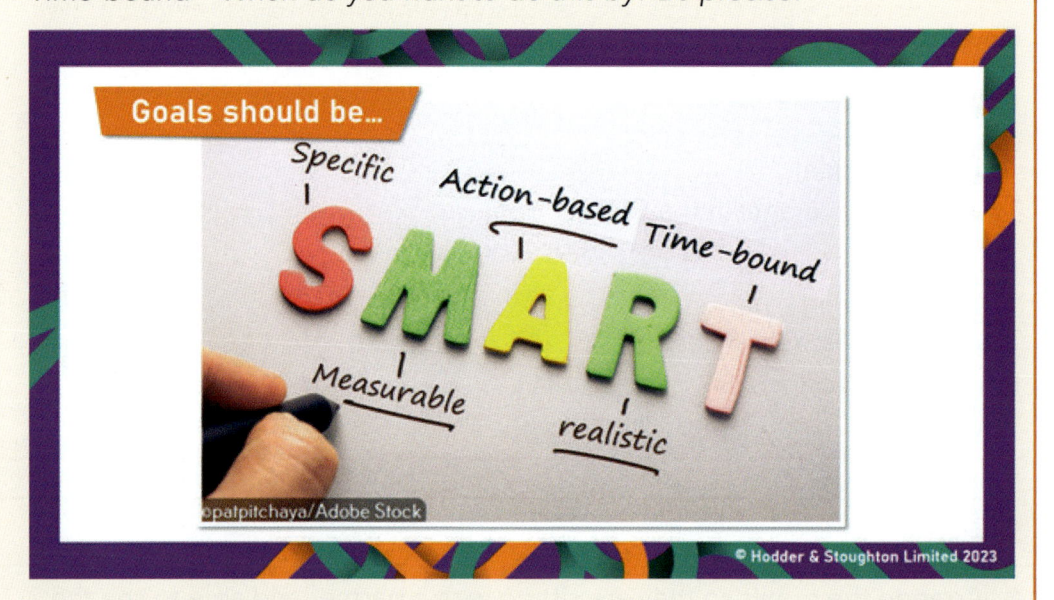

7. Model to the pupils breaking down an example goal into a SMART goal. This process is vital as sharing the visible thinking will support pupils in setting their own goals.

   Goal – I want to improve my reading

Specific	I want to improve my reading and be able to answer complex questions and score 110 in my test.
Measurable	I will know as I will have read two books every week. I will know as I will answer the complex questions correctly. I will know as I will score 110.
Action-based	I will read more books. I will practise answering complex questions at home. I will ask my teacher for help.
Realistic	I can do this as I know others have worked hard and achieved this.
Time-bound	I will have achieved this by May.

8. Ask the pupils to think about:

   What goal do you want to achieve?

9. Provide the pupils with some thinking time and then develop their thinking further.
10. Ask them to create their own SMART goal. Share with the pupils the **handout** and then ask them to make their goal into a SMART goal.
11. Give the pupils time and support any pupils who need help breaking their goal down into a SMART goal.
12. Once they have completed their SMART goals, ask some pupils to share their goals using a visualiser.
13. Remind the pupils that it is challenging to set SMART goals and that they should practise doing this and set a SMART goal every week.

Follow up

Revisit the pupils' SMART goals and ask them to review them regularly. Regularly ask the pupils to set SMART goals so they can practise this approach.

Pupils' responses

What does the word 'goal' mean?

> 'You can have a goal in life, for example to climb a mountain or get better at something.'

> 'A target to do something.'

> 'An achievement.'

> 'Something that you aim for.'

What goal do you want to achieve?

Goal- I want to improve my French.

Specific	I want to be able to fluently speak French by being able to have a full conversation.
Measurable	I will try and revise what I already know in french.
Action-based	Ask parent for help (or teacher) Go on Duolingo (language learning app)
Realistic	I know people have achieved this.
Time Bound	I will try and achieve this by the time I start Year 7

Goal- Get better at lacrosse.

Specific	To get better at lacrosse and play better, and get better at defence.
Measurable	I will try play lacrosse in my garden everyday and I will get better.
Action-based	I will try listen more in training and I will also practise my shooting.
Realistic	I know other people have achieved this.
Time Bound	I will get better by September.

Goal- I want to improve my coding

Specific	I want to improve my coding by being able to code a single game to show my friends.
Measurable	I will learn to move the character I will also try to add some enemys
Action-based	I will ask my parents to help I will watch multiple tutorials and play other games for inspiration
Realistic	I know others that others have achieved
Time Bound	I will achieve this by 2023

Pupils' SMART goals

8 Inner critic

Summary

This session encourages pupils to reflect on their own inner critic and its impact, and to explore how an alternative voice can support them.

Focus

Developing control, challenge, commitment and confidence

Outcome

To explore strategies to help pupils deal with their negative critic

To challenge their critic and change negative messages into positive messages

Resources

Teaching slides: Year 6 Session 8
Sticky notes

Session

1. Arrange the pupils so they are sitting with a partner and can see the board.
2. Share with the pupils the negative vocabulary on the **first teaching slide** and read it together.

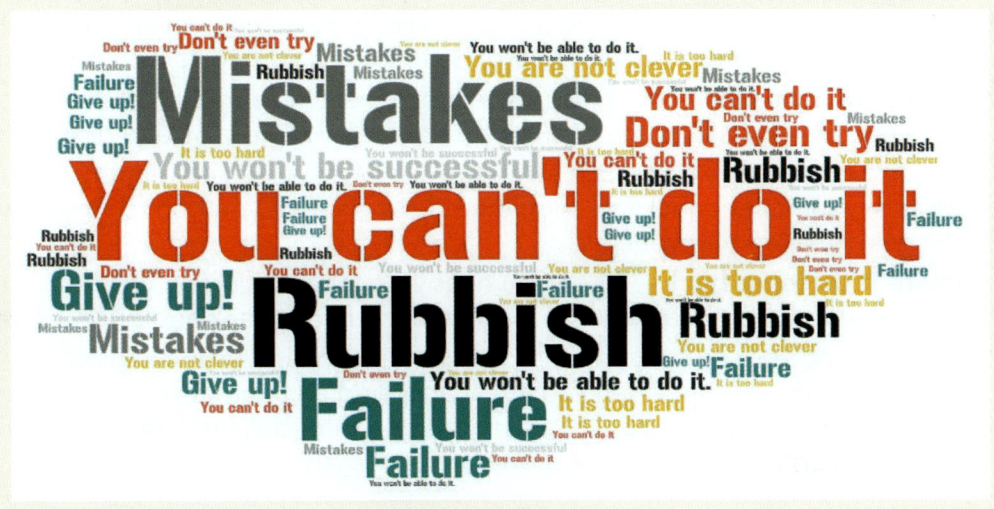

Then ask the pupils to reflect on:

How does this make you feel?

3. Take feedback from the pupils and then share the image of their inner critic on the **next teaching slide**.

Inner Critic

4. Explain to the pupils that we all have an inner critic – a voice inside of us that is negative and criticises us. Often it prevents us from doing things as it tells us that we can't do things. Everyone has an inner critic, even the most successful people; they just develop strategies to deal with it.

5. Model something that your inner critic often says to you and share with the pupils how this makes you feel.

6. Ask the pupils to think about something their inner critic regularly says and to write it down on a sticky note. If a pupil can't think of something, suggest something they might say.

7. Explain to the pupils that there are strategies that we can develop to deal with our inner voice positively. Share the following strategies with the class:

   Name it – By naming your inner voice it can make it seem silly and not as valuable. Give it a silly name and use that to help you devalue and dismiss it.

   Listen and reframe – You can listen to your inner voice and identify it for what is, your inner critic! You should not let it prevent you from doing new things or challenging yourself.

   Invite it to come back – When you hear your inner critic, you can acknowledge it but state that you will listen to it in a week and push it away.

   Model using your own example of your inner critic and how it can be reframed. Ensure that, when you are scaffolding an alternative, you don't just remove the contraction, e.g. change 'don't' to 'do'. Instead, you should change the phrasing to have a more positive focus.

Visible Thinking

My inner critic says that I am not very good at writing, but I know that I have improved and that I can write great explanations.

8 Ask the pupils to reframe what their inner critic says in a positive way:
   How can you reframe your inner critic?
   Encourage them to use evidence from previous experiences when they have been successful.
   Ask any pupils who are willing to share how they have reframed their inner critic.

9 Provide the pupils with some time to reflect on:
   Which of the strategies are you going to try? Why?

10 Take feedback from the pupils and gather their opinions.

11 Ask the pupils:
   Are there any other strategies you could use?

Follow up

Revisit the concept of the inner critic and ask the pupils to reflect on how they are approaching it.

Create a class display with prompts to support pupils in challenging their inner critic.

Pupils' responses

How does this make you feel?
- '*Negative.*'
- '*Upset.*'
- '*Like you can't do anything.*'
- '*Annoyed – if someone said it to you as they don't think you can do things.*'

How can you reframe your inner critic?
- '*That looks messy – Try to make it neater.*'
- '*Don't try – Have a go, you can do it!*'
- '*You will fail – Have a go, you are learning to do it.*'

Which of the strategies are you going to try? Why?
- '*Reframing – as it makes it sound better.*'
- '*Name it – as it makes me laugh! I'll be too busy laughing.*'
- '*Sending it away – although it will come back.*'
- '*Using all three will be most effective.*'

References

Alexander, C. (2021). *A Little Bit Different*. London: Happy Yak.

Andreae, G., & Parker-Rees, G. (2014). *Giraffes Can't Dance*. London: Orchard Books.

Blackwell, L., Trzesniewski, K., & Dweck, C.S. (2007). Implicit theories of intelligence predict achievement across an adolescent transition: A longitudinal study and an intervention. *Child Development*, 78(1), 246–263.

Bowles, S., & Gintis, H. (1976). *Schooling in Capitalist America*. New York: Basic Books.

Byers, G. (2020). *I Believe I Can*. New York: Balzer & Bray.

Clarke, S. (2014). *Outstanding Formative Assessment: Culture and Practice*. London: Hodder Education.

Clough, P.J., Earle, K., & Sewell, D. (2002). Mental toughness: The concept and its measurement. In Cockerill, I. (Ed.), *Solutions in Sport Psychology* (pp. 32–43). London: Thomson Publishers.

Clough, P., Oakes, S., Dagnall, N., St Clair-Thompson, H., & McGeown, S. (2016). The Study of Non-cognitive Attributes in Education: Proposing the Mental Toughness Framework. In Khine, M.S., & Areepattamannil, S. (Eds), *Non-cognitive Skills and Factors in Educational Achievement* (pp. 315–329). Rotterdam: Sense Publishers.

Credé, M., Tynan, M.C., & Harms, P.D. (2017). Much ado about grit: A meta-analytic synthesis of the grit literature. *Journal of Personality and Social Psychology*, 113(3), 492–511.

Crust, L. (2008). A review and conceptual re-examination of mental toughness: Implications for future researchers. *Personality and Individual Differences*, 45(7), 576–583.

Dawson, A., Yeomans, E., & Brown, E.R. (2018). Methodological challenges in education RCTs: Reflections from England's Education Endowment Foundation. *Educational Research*, 60(3), 292–310.

Department for Education (2019). *Changes to personal, social, health and economic (PSHE) and relationships and sex education (RSE)*. Retrieved 11 November 2022 from www.gov.uk/government/publications/changes-to-personal-social-health-and-economic-pshe-and-relationships-and-sex-education-rse

DiTerlizzi, A. (2020). *The Magical Yet*. Glendale: Disney-Hyperion.

Duckworth, A.L., Peterson, C., Matthews, M.D., & Kelly, D.R. (2007). Grit: Perseverance and passion for long-term goals. *Journal of Personality and Social Psychology*, 92, 1087–1101.

Duckworth, A.L., & Yeager, D. (2015). Measurement matters: Assessing Personal Qualities Other Than Cognitive Ability for Educational Purposes. *Educational*

Researcher, 44(4), 237–251. Retrieved 11 November 2022 from www.jstor.org/stable/24571517.

Dweck, C.S. (2006). *Mindset: The new psychology of success*. New York: Random House Publishing.

Dweck, C.S. (2015). Carol Dweck revisits the growth mindset. *Education Week*, 35(5), 20–24.

Farrington, C.A., Roderick, M., Allensworth, E., Nagaoka, J., Keyes, T.S., Johnson, D.W., & Beechum, N.O. (2012). *Teaching adolescents to become learners. The role of non-cognitive factors in shaping school performance: A critical literature review*. University of Chicago: Consortium on Chicago School Research.

Foliano, F., Rolfe, H., Buzzeo, J., Runge, J., & Wilkinson, D. (2019). *Changing Mindsets: Effectiveness Trial*. Education Endowment Foundation. Retrieved 11 November 2022 from www.niesr.ac.uk/wp-content/uploads/2021/10/Changing-Mindsets_0-4.pdf

Fraser, L., & Hindley, K. (2020). *The Littlest Yak*. London: Simon & Schuster Children's Books.

Gerber, M., Brand, S., Feldmeth, A.K., Lang, C., Elliot, C., Holsboer-Trachsler, E., & Pühse, U. (2013). Adolescents with high mental toughness adapt better to perceived stress: A longitudinal study with Swiss vocational students. *Personality and Individual Differences*, 54, 808–814.

Golby, J., Sheard, M., & van Wersch, A. (2007). Evaluating the factor structure of the psychological performance inventory. *Perceptual and Motor Skills*, 1(105), 309–325.

Gucciardi, D.F., Gordon, S., & Dimmock, J.A. (2008). Towards an understanding of mental toughness in Australian football. *Journal of Applied Sport Psychology*, 3(20), 261–281.

Gucciardi, D.F., Gordon, S., & Dimmock, J.A. (2009). Evaluation of a Mental Toughness Training Program for Youth-Aged Australian Footballers: A Quantitative Analysis. *Journal of Applied Sport Psychology*, 3(21), 307–323.

Gutman, L.M., & Schoon, I. (2013). *The impact of non-cognitive skills on outcomes for young people*. Education Endowment Foundation. Retrieved 11 November 2022 from https://educationendowmentfoundation.org.uk/public/files/Presentations/Publications/Non-cognitive_skills_literature_review_1.pdf

Heckman, J.J., & Kautz, T. (2012). Hard evidence on soft skills. *Labour Economics*, 19(4), 451–464.

Lin, Y., Mutz, J., Clough, P.J., & Papageorgiou, K.A. (2017). Mental toughness and individual differences in learning, educational and work performance, psychological well-being, and personality: A systematic review. *Frontiers in Psychology*, 8. Article 1345.

Luyken, C. (2017). *The Book of Mistakes*. New York: Rocky Pond Books.

McGeown, S.P., St Clair-Thompson, H., Clough, P. (2015). The study of non-cognitive attributes in education: Proposing the Mental Toughness Framework. *Educational Review*, 1(68), 13–96.

McGeown, S., Clair-Thompson, H., & Putwain, D.W. (2016). The development and validation of a mental toughness scale for adolescents. *Journal of Psychoeducational Assessment,* 2(36), 148–161.

Miçooğullari, B.O., & Ekmekçi, R. (2017). Evaluation of a psychological skill training program on mental toughness and psychological wellbeing for professional soccer players. *Universal Journal of Educational Research,* 5(12), 2312–2319.

Muncaster, K., & Clarke, S. (2016). *Growth Mindset Lessons: Every Child a Learner.* London: Rising Stars UK Limited.

Negley, K. (2019). *Tough Guys (Have Feelings Too).* London: Flying Eye Books.

Percival, T. (2021). *Tilda Tries Again: A Big Bright Feelings Book.* London: Bloomsbury Children's Books.

Slack, L.A., Maynard, I., Butt, J., & Olusoga, P. (2015). An evaluation of a mental toughness education and training program for early-career English football league referees. *Sports Psychologist,* 29(3), 237–257.

Stamp, E., Crust, L., Swann, C., Perry, J., Clough, P., & Marchant, D. (2015). Relationships between mental toughness and psychological wellbeing in undergraduate students. *Personality and Individual Differences*, (75), 170–174.

Stankov, L., & Lee, J. (2014). Quest for the best non-cognitive predictor of academic achievement. *Educational Psychology,* 1(34), 1–8.

St Clair-Thompson, H., Bugler, M., Robinson, J., McGeown, S., Perry, J., & Clough, P. (2015). Mental toughness in education: Exploring relationships with attainment, attendance, behaviour and peer relationships. *Educational Psychology: An International Journal of Experimental Educational Psychology*, 7(35), 886–907.

St Clair-Thompson, H., Giles, R., McGeown, S.P., Putwain, D., Clough, P., & Perry, J. (2017). Mental toughness and transitions to high school and to undergraduate study. *Educational Psychology,* 37(7), 792–809.

Strycharczyk, D., & Clough, P. (2018). *Developing Mental Toughness in Young People.* London: Routledge.

Tomlinson, J. (2014) *The Owl Who was Afraid of the Dark.* London: HarperCollins.

White, R.E., Prager, E.O., Schaefer, C., Kross, E., Duckworth, A.L., & Carlson, S.M. (2016). The 'Batman Effect': Improving perseverance in young children. *Child Development,* 5(88), 1563–1571.

Winfield Martin, E. (2015). *The Wonderful Things You Will Be.* New York: Random House Young Readers.

Yeager, D.S., Hanselman, P., Walton, G.M., Murray, J.S., Crosnoe, R., Muller, C., Paunesku, D., Romero, C., Flint, K., Roberts, A., Trott, J., Iachan, R., Buontempo, J., Man Yang, S., Carvalho, C.M., Hahn, R.P., Gopalan, M., Mhatre, P., Feguson, R., Duckworth, A.L., Dweck, C.S. (2019). A national experiment reveals where a growth mindset improves achievement. *Nature,* 573, 364–369.